The Journey

40 Days of Prophetic Mentorship

BRYAN MEADOWS

Copyright © 2014 by Bryan Meadows

All rights reserved.

All rights reserved. No part of this publication may be reproduced, distributed, or transmitted in any form or by any means, including photocopying, recording, or other electronic or mechanical methods, without the prior written permission of the publisher, except in the case of brief quotations embodied in critical reviews and certain other noncommercial uses permitted by copyright law. For permission requests, write to the publisher, addressed "Attention: Permissions Coordinator," at the address below.

BRYAN MEADOWS MINISTRIES

P.O. Box 161221

Atlanta, Georgia 30321

ISBN-13: 978-1494980245

ISBN-10: 149498024X

All artwork done by Grant Edwards

Grant.Edwards@ymail.com

All Editing and Formatting done by Stephanie Anderson of Scribez LLC Editing Services Smyrna, GA. ScribezLLC@gmail.com

All scripture quotations, unless otherwise indicated, are taken from the King James Version (Authorized Version). First published in 1611.

Table of Contents

Dedication *5*

The Mystery of Mentorship *7*

How to Use this Book *11*

The Journey: 40 Days of Prophetic Mentorship

Session One / *Past* / 13

Session Two / *Preparation* / 33

Session Three / *Potential* / 55

Session Four / *Purpose* / 77

Session Five / *Power* / 99

Session Six / *Personality* / 125

Session Seven / *Price* / 147

Session Eight / *Presence* / 169

THE JOURNEY

DEDICATION

I would like to dedicate this book to the Leadership Team of Embassy International Worship Center. In 2011 we started in my living room with a simple vision: to build God something He would be proud of. In the process of building something great for God, we became more than a team... we became family. We love you all from the bottom of my heart. Lady Patrice and I see your dedication, sacrifice, and hard work. I pray for you all with my whole heart. I believe in you. I wouldn't want to do life with any other group of people. Thank you for allowing us to pastor you. It is truly an honor and a privilege. Let's change the world!

THE JOURNEY

The Mystery of Mentorship

While mentorship seems to be the latest spiritual fad, this ancient discipline has never lost its place in our faith. The art of walking alongside an individual, in both knowledge and presence, for the purpose of pulling out ones potential is relevant now more than ever. In a day where being gifted is normal, and savants sit on every street, why does it seem as if the problems of the 21st Century are steadily getting worse? Out of all these minds, can we still not find a solution? We are not circus performers, gathering just to be awed by our uniqueness. We are citizens of the Kingdom of God raised up to establish Christ and His culture in our communities. Our purpose as Believers is to make an impact. But how do we move from philosophy to power? For the Kingdom of God is not found in philosophy, but in the demonstration of power. How do we move from rhetoric to reality? Moving a gift from potential to potency is a process.

Every gift requires a process. It's the process of mentorship. Mentorship is the vehicle that takes your gift from infancy to solution. Paul tells the church of Corinth "do not be ignorant of spiritual gifts ..." Paul does not give us a dissertation or even a demonstration of those gifts, he merely names them. These gifts were so normal, so frequent, so common in the first century church that Paul needed only mention them, and everyone understood what he meant. But like the church at Corinth, their immaturity in the gifts produced the very opposite of the gift's purpose. The gifts were meant to bring people together, to strengthen and edify the Body. But their immaturity in the gifts of the Spirit caused division, and actually weakened the Church. Well, what is the bridge between immaturity and maturity? Mentorship!

Some would say life is the greatest teacher. And while life is a great teacher, this statement is incomplete. If we all enrolled in the University of Life, which is a 30 year program, complete with failures, bad decisions, lost time, broken hearts, and debt, we would all begin where our parents began. Sadly, too many generations are cursed to start from the beginning because of the inability to pass down wisdom and knowledge. What if there was a private institution that accelerated our learning? What if there was a divine program designed to strategically give you what you needed for your destiny? There is something supernatural that happens in the process of mentorship. When a person goes through life they gain knowledge and experience. When knowledge and experience looks backwards, this produces wisdom. Wisdom is grown in time. The mystery of Mentorship is that a mentee can live vicariously through their mentor. A mentor shares their experiences and knowledge so that the student can bypass generic mistakes and demonic traps designed to decelerate the rate of success. The model of mentorship can be seen all throughout scripture. We see it in the life of Elijah and Elisha, Paul and Timothy, and of course with Jesus and the Disciples.

Through tutelage God established a system of impartation. Mentorship has always been God's vehicle to pass down revelation, wisdom, and knowledge. In the Church, this system is called discipleship. When one first comes into the Kingdom of God there is a transitionary period called sanctification. Sanctification is the process of burying the old man, along with his habits, culture, and conversation. The ability to remove previous perceptions, adapt news ones, and implement a new lifestyle isn't easy. It takes guidance, counsel, coaching, and leadership to get from one level to the next. Mentorship is the strategic education of a person for purpose. Mentorship is the apprenticeship for world changers. Mentorship gives us the ability to redeem time. The time that our parents lost through mistakes we can buy back through their wisdom by utilizing their experiences and knowledge to make better choices. Mentorship creates a model for students to observe and use as a tool to measure success.

Mentorship can come in a variety of ways. Mentorship can be very indirect, for example books, messages, television, and even mutual relationships represent indirect forms of mentorship. Or mentorship can be very personal, through quality time, laying on of hands, moments, or prophecy. All levels of mentorship are designed to increase your life in a distinct way. Mentoring requires time. Time is the greatest commodity in the mentorship process. God has given every man a measure of days. For someone to sow their time into you is a precious thing. Time is a non-replenishable commodity, just like coal or petroleum. Every Believer must see value in submission. Submission is seen many times as subjugation. True submission is an investment of time. When you submit yourself to a mentor, it is because you have the ability to discern your worth.

The fact that you have picked up this program means that you understand the power of investment. You apparently know your worth. for it is only those who understand their worth, that will subject themselves to mentorship. Get ready for a journey of edification, stretching, and perfecting. You have been targeted for greatness, now you must take the journey!

THE HOW TO

Welcome to The Journey. The Journey is a 40 Day Mentorship course designed to push you to your spiritual limits. This program was birthed from a course we did with over 200 students. For 40 days we challenged eight specific areas of development. The results of The Journey were mind blowing. What started as a small mentorship class morphed into an international movement. We witnessed people from over 30 of our 50 states, and more than six nations participate. The Journey is a unique mentorship course that you may complete at your own pace. This program is built with four goals in mind:

1. Stretch ones potential, opening up a whole new world of opportunities.
2. Address limitations, weaknesses, habits, and tendencies that inhibit growth and development.
3. Locate and articulate assignments and their measures for more accurate and efficient ministry.
4. Establish and affirm rank and file among gifts, with a focus on order, protocol, and the implementation of strategy.

The Journey consists of eight sessions, which are all five days each. Each day you will receive INSPIRATION, MEDITATION, and ACTIVATION for the purpose of Kingdom development.

INSPIRATION: Your inspiration will be a prophetic word, wisdom, a proverb, dark saying, or decree. This is meant to direct the prophetic affairs of your daily dealings, as well as edify your spirit and intellect. This section is meant to encourage, confirm, and strengthen you daily. Each day of this program is equipped with a portion of inspiration. Inspiration is defined as the process of being cerebrally stimulated to do or feel something, especially to do something creative or original. This portion of the mentorship journey is created to motivate and breathe life into you. The word inspire literally means to inhale. It is in this prophetic section that God breathes life into you, all you have to do is breathe in. Inhaling denotes accepting. Everyday in this section you will receive inspiration that's molded to make you better, but it only works by your acceptance.

MEDITATION: Meditation is the process of moving information from the mind to the heart. In this section we will be introducing new concepts, ideas, and themes for the purpose of stretching your perspective. This section will require more than your mere attention. This section requires action. Meditation is very active. The power of meditation is in repetition. This section is designed to both instruct and inspire. You will need to harness the powers of discipline, memorization, and timing to be successful in this portion. Your meditation is purposed to interrupt your current thought pattern, and address the rhythm of your thinking. This will usually come in the form of a concept, quote, and a scripture reading for the day. This is meant to target your intercessory activity and your confessions. In order to get the full experience from the meditation portion, we recommend 5-10 minutes of quiet time as you complete this exercise.

ACTIVATION: This is very unique. Your activation will be an actual duty that you are to perform or an activity that you are challenged to engage in. Everyday you will receive a prophetic instruction. For example: (Prophesy to the first person you see at work) and you will journal your experience. This is meant to train your obedience, sharpen your gifts, amplify your hearing, and increase your measure.

THE JOURNEY

Session One: Your Past

DAY 1

💡 INSPIRATION

In 1 Kings 17, we are introduced to Elijah. The scripture calls him a Tishbite, but at no time does it tell us where Elijah came from, besides his geographical location. We don't know his spiritual lineage. We don't know if his father was a prophet. We don't know what he has been through, BUT TRUST ME, Elijah does. Just because you don't know what I went through to get the oil that's on my life, rest assured … I PAID A PRICE!!! It is NOT always important that others know what you've been through, but it is of utmost importance that YOU KNOW what you've been through. When Elijah shows up on the scene, he is already doing great things for God. Many times when we see people doing great things for God, we have a tendency to forget that they've been through Hell to get what's on their life. All of us are products of our past. If it's one thing that connects all of humanity, it is a past … we all have one. Some are proud of their past, others not so much. But regardless of our perspective, our past has power. The past offers us a unique perspective. The past is the mirror for our development. The past shows us how we have grown, or reminds us of how we've remained the same. How do you know where you've been, without looking back from where you've come from? How much distance have you covered? **Some people forfeit the potency of their anointing by ignoring the purpose in their past.** There is purpose in your past, no matter how dark, dirty, or distorted it may seem. Confess this: THERE IS PURPOSE IN MY PAST (repeat 7 times aloud). Where did you come from? What have you been through? Who are you really?

MEDITATION

Where did I come from? Now that is a great question to ask! What if I told you that the anointing, the gift, and even the promise of God over your life has travelled generations to reach you. What you're carrying on your life did not just appear out of thin air. God used everyone that came before you, their life, hardships, and even failures, to make sure that what's on your life was purposeful and potent.

Concept: THE ANOINTING TRAVELS (Psalm 133)

Here are some questions to ponder:
1. Where did I come from?
2. What were the circumstances surrounding my birth?
3. Where did my GIFTS come from? Does anyone in my family have my gift and/or a similar assignment?
4. What has been the journey of my anointing?

Scripture Reading
1 Kings 17:1, Hebrews 7:1-3, Matthew 1:1-17

ACTIVATION

Your Prophetic exercise today is to make a list. Think back, as far as you can remember (this may require some investigation, like asking family members) and track the anointing on your life. Anointings can be imparted through **PEOPLE, PLACES,** and **PROBLEMS**. Each person, place, and problem that the anointing went through to get to you, added another piece of the prophetic puzzle that makes your gifting unique. Make a list of every **PERSON, PLACE,** and **PROBLEM**, that you can remember, that had a direct affect in shaping the anointing on your life.

Day 2

💡 INSPIRATION

Everything that God creates has value. God created time. This is important to understand. Time is a created thing. It is tangible. It can be felt, measured, loss, spent, gained, bought, and traded. Time is power. When God created Adam, he was timeless. Adam was made in God's image and likeness … HE WAS ETERNAL. Adam didn't need a watch. He was a being of destiny and purpose. Adam was not bound by time. Adam did not become subject to time until he fell. After Genesis chapter 3, man became a slave of time. Since Adam's treason, we have been incarcerated by time. Once Adam fell, he began to age, and there was nothing he could do about it. Look what Job said,

Man that is born of a woman is of few days, and full of trouble. (**Job 14:1**)

Adam lived until he was 930 years old … just a few days. Time is limited. Anything limited, is extremely valuable. Time is valuable. Anything that is valuable, has an appraised worth. Appraised worth is when value is revealed through a controlled system. How do you appraise the worth of your time? Take an appraisal of your time. When worth is not attached to time, you give it away freely. Understand, time is an ever appreciating commodity. TIME NEVER LOSES VALUE. This is why one of the most heinous crimes in the Kingdom of God is the wasting of time. Wasting time is the ultimate form of disrespect. Time wasters are destiny killers. Time wasters are purpose assassins. Why? Because all you have is time. TIME IS VALUABLE. You will be a person that values time. PRAY THIS PRAYER ALOUD:

Father, teach me to value time. Give me revelation of every time block. Give me revelation of the past, present, and future. Father, I value time. Lord, teach me how to manage the time you've given me. Teach me how to use the time I have wisely. Father any time I have wasted, lost, misplaced, or forfeited, redeem now in Jesus' name. Amen. CONFESS THIS: My time is valuable (repeat 7 times aloud).

Most people put value on the present. They believe that the only time that is important, is the time they have right now. Others, put much value on the future. They are excited about what is "going to happen". Today we are going to add value to our time. Did you know there is value in your past? The past is not just a platform for our testimonies. The past is not just a season you survived. **Our past is an ever teaching instructor furiously focused on making us better.** God is NOT a God of waste. God is a God of purpose. God is intentional, and nothing that God does is ever extraneous. Our past is never wasted. God takes every second, minute, day . . . every measurement of time spent in the past, and turns them into lessons that we can never lose. Don't try to forget the past, add value to it by taking note of what you learned, and how you grew. Time requires revelation. Without revelation, every second seems the same. But when time meets revelation, a moment is created. Once you get revelation of your past, value is added to it, and you realize that nothing you went through was superfluous.

 MEDITATION

In 1952, in his book *Relativity*, in discussing Minkowski's Space World interpretation of his theory of relativity, Albert Einstein writes:

"Since there exists in this four dimensional structure [space-time] no longer any sections which represent "now" objectively, the concepts of happening and becoming are indeed not completely suspended, but yet complicated. It appears therefore more natural to think of physical reality as a four dimensional existence, instead of, as hitherto, the evolution of a three dimensional existence."

Albert Einstein discovered the concept known as space-time. He said that the world that we live in was not just three-dimensional, but four-dimensional. He added time to space. 4 dimensions: height, width, depth, and time. Einstein believed that TIME WAS TANGIBLE. He believed time could be bent, manipulated, stretched, and even travelled.

Concept: SPACE-TIME. Time is integrated into our space. TIME IS TANGIBLE (Joel 2:25)

Here are some things to ponder:
1. How much is my time worth?
2. How much would I pay to spend time with me?
3. How valuable is my minute?
4. Am I a time waster? If so, how do I waste time?

Scripture Reading:
Eccl. 3:11, Job 14:1-14, Acts 1:6-8

ACTIVATION

Create a schedule that you will abide by for the next 7 days. Create a detailed schedule of your day. Plan your productivity. In this schedule, include morning prayer, The JOURNEY, reading the Word of God, some worship time, and some exercise. After that, you can integrate it with your regular schedule. But make sure every hour is accounted for. For 7 days, stick to this schedule religiously. Plan your breakfast, reading, and even recreational time. As you do this, your minute will mature.

Notes

DAY 3

💡 INSPIRATION

Our past is the canvas upon which God paints a masterpiece called redemption. The deeper the grave, the greater the resurrection. Our future is called destiny. Our present is called reality. But our past is called history. History is defined as the study of past events. What is your HISTORY with God? Throughout the scripture you'll encounter men who "walked" with God. The word "walk" is synonymous with the word "live". This literally means that they had LIFE WITH God. The scripture says that Enoch "walked" with God. In Genesis chapter 3, we see God going to "walk" with Adam in the cool of the day. God wants to take a walk with you. God is not a general who barks orders just to see who will disobey so that He can have a reason to unleash His wrath. God is a father, a friend … He is raw favor. God is looking for someone to bless. Now here is an important lesson. A blessing is not just the object received, or the promise manifested … a blessing is the process by which the promise or object is given. To bless means to empower. Has your past taught you anything? If it has, that means that your past has empowered you. DID YOU GET THAT? Your past, no matter how dark and dank … IS. A. BLESSING! Can you say that with me? Confess this: MY PAST IS BLESSING ME RIGHT NOW (repeat 7 times aloud).

God wants to build history with you. He is not threatened by your famines or phobias. God is not intimidated by your weaknesses or failures. God wants to live with you, and NOT just in the good times. Can I tell you a secret? God is addicted to drama! He loves situations that boggle the human mind and challenge the heart . . . GOD IS

BUILT FOR YOUR BAD MOMENTS. He loves being around during the messy times of your life, just to see you through to victory. God is a show off. His ultimate performance was the death, burial, and resurrection of His son. Do you know the look on Hell's face when the man, the prophet, the "Messiah" they thought they had embarrassed and humiliated, suddenly got up from the dead? All of creation froze, all of Heaven stood to attention, all of Hell shrunk in fear … HE IS ALIVE. Regardless of your situation right now, regardless of your past, your reputation, the most unspeakable mistakes … Can I prophesy to you and say when this is over, Heaven will shout, "HE IS ALIVE!!! SHE IS ALIVE!!!" Our past is our badge of honor. OUR past is OUR proof that OUR God has ALL power!

MEDITATION

Concept: The Sovereignty of God (**Ephesians 1:6-16**)

The sovereignty of God is hard to understand, especially when we are limited to a "free will" perspective. A.W. Tozer attempted to reconcile these seemingly contradictory ideas of God choosing or calling us and our choosing God with this illustration:

"An ocean liner leaves New York bound for Liverpool. Its destination has been determined by proper authorities. Nothing can change it. This is at least a faint picture of sovereignty. On board the liner are scores of passengers. These are not in chains, neither are their activities determined for them by decree. They are completely free to move about as they will. They eat, sleep, play, lounge about on the deck, read, talk, altogether as they please; but all the while the great liner is carrying them steadily onward toward a predetermined port (which they have accepted as their destination). Both freedom and sovereignty are present here, and they do not contradict. So it is, I believe, with man's freedom and the sovereignty

of God. The mighty liner of God's sovereign design keeps its steady course over the sea of history."

Take a moment a ponder on the sovereignty of God. Think about all that God has done and provided in SPITE OF what we did to NOT deserve it. Think about the fact that while there may be drama on the boat … it can't change the destination.

Scripture Reading:
Gen. 5:24, Josh. 4:1-8, Luke 24:1-18

ACTIVATION

God wants to build history with you! In the days of Old, saints of El Elyon (The Most High God) would build history with God by building memorials. After a great victory, an amazing encounter, an unforgettable experience, they would erect a stone, a pillar, or even dig a well of water. Can you remember some great moments you've had with God? How did they develop you? What was their lasting impression? In Genesis chapter 22, Abraham has an encounter with God where God reveals Himself as Jehovah Jireh. Abraham, after this experience, named the place where He was Jehovah Jireh. He recorded the name of the Lord in that place, so that he would never forget what God did. Take a few moments to RECOUNT and RECORD 7 encounters with the Lord that literally changed your life. Include where you were, what happened, who was with you, and what developed in your life as a result of it.

DAY 4

INSPIRATION

God is a God of generations. We hear God refer to Himself many times as the God of Abraham, Isaac, and Jacob. God doesn't just want to be involved in the "here and now". Our God has committed to your now, your later, and guess what ... God has committed to your past! It is interesting that God would refer to Himself as the God of Abraham, Isaac, and Jacob. Abraham was a great man. I understand God's affinity towards Abraham ... look what Abraham did. By a word, *Genesis chapter 12*, Abraham left everything to walk with God. There is no wonder why Abraham becomes God's friend. Isaac! I even understand God saying that He's the "God of Isaac!" Isaac sacrificed much. He was willing, *Genesis chapter 22*, to allow His father to tie him up and kill him, all because "GOD SAID SO!" That is a major sacrifice. But Jacob! Jacob was a mess up from the beginning. From the time we are introduced to Jacob in scripture, his mother is already devising a plan to steal the birthright ... Isaac is dying, and his older brother Esau is doing all the work for the house. Jacob is a mess! Jacob steals the birthright and begins to run from his past. Jacob's life is characterized by running. He never deals with issues... he just runs away.

The past is not something you can run from. Its omnipresent power has a way of following you wherever you go. The past can be an unrelenting stalker bent on burying you in guilt and stealing the power of the present moment. You can move to another state, get a new job, even remarry ... that doesn't deal with the past. The past must be CONFRONTED. The past doesn't disappear just because you "move on"... it lingers like legal cases until every legality is addressed and dealt with.

Accepting the past can be the hardest thing to do when you are moving forward. You must be able, without giving an excuse, to look at your mistakes and say, "YES, IT HAPPENED, I DID IT, WHAT DO I DO NOW?" This can be the hardest part of deliverance ... TAKING RESPONSIBILITY.

STOP EVERYTHING!!! I know this might be hard, but repeat after me: IT. WAS. MY. FAULT! (repeat 7 times aloud)

In Genesis, chapter 3, after Adam and Eve sinned, God comes looking for them. Of course when He finds them, they are hiding behind trees, because sin will always RELOCATE you. After a brief conversation, Adam blames his wife for the mishap. Eve blames the serpent. And since the serpent had no one else to blame, he was the first to be cursed. Blame activates curses. **When you fail to take responsibility for your past, grace is neutralized, shame grows, and your integrity begins to decay.** Jacob at some point had to face his past. At some point you get tired of running. At some point you get tired of lying. At some point you get tired of hiding it. YOU'VE GOT TO BE FREE! Every one of us must get to this point before breakthrough occurs. Jacob reaches his limit, and he decides to stop running and confront his past. Jacob doesn't just face the issue, he grabs hold of it, and begins to wrestle. The past must be wrestled with. Don't sit down and have a tea party with your past. Get in the ring with your past, and make a declaration ... "Only one of us is leaving here alive!"

And Jacob was left alone; and there wrestled a man with him until the breaking of the day. (**Gen. 32:24**)

Notice that Jacob wrestled until the "breaking of day." The word "day" in Hebrew, is the word *YOM*. It literally means the period of time that light is released. It is a moment of revelation. Jacob wrestled with his past until he got revelation. Do not stop wrestling with your past until you extract every drop of revelation out of it. SQEEZE your past until you get every lesson, every drop of oil, every testimony. SQUEEZE your past until you get stronger, wiser, richer, and better.

MEDITATION

Concept: Taking Responsibility (**1 Cor. 13:11**)

We've all done childish things. But when we mature, we have a responsibility to put away those things that made us children. Today, ponder on the concept of taking responsibility. Great leaders always take the blame. Today we are making a commitment to never blame another person for the actions and decisions we make. I wasn't tricked, duped, or forced into a bad situation … I MADE A DECISION. Take a moment and meditate on the new, mature, responsible you. What does he look like? What does she look like? In what areas can you step up? In what areas can you begin to take responsibility?

Questions to ask yourself. PLEASE ANSWER HONESTLY:
1. Am I afraid of responsibility?
2. Is there anything in my life I am afraid of people finding out?
3. Am I a dishonest person?
4. How often do I lie, embellish, fabricate, or twist facts?
5. What am I running from?

These questions, as you meditate, and answer them, will unlock a new level of responsibility in your life. LIVE ON PURPOSE!

THE JOURNEY

Scripture Reading:
Gen. 3, Gen. 25, John 9:1-3

ACTIVATION

As you meditate, create a list of situations, problems, and/or circumstances that you know were undeniably your fault. Include at least 3 major situations, and 2 minor ones. Dissect the situation, think about what you would do differently, journal what you learned through the experience, and then write down what you would do differently if you could do it again, and "I WOULDN'T DO ANYTHING DIFFERENTLY" is NOT an option. Create an alternative path. This is exercising your wisdom!

Notes

Day 5

 INSPIRATION

Jesus, after He is baptized, and initiated into His earthly ministry, goes and begins to teach within the Jewish synagogues. Jesus was an absolutely astounding gift. He taught with much authority (**Matt. 7:29**). While He wasn't the only preacher, the only leader, the only one to grace the pulpit, there was something different about His confidence, His swagger, His boldness and security. When Jesus takes the platform, He turns to the book of Isaiah, chapter 61, and begins to read. The entire congregation is wondering what is happening. This looks like a normal moment, but something is different about this day. Jesus, with a thundering voice says, "The Spirit of the Lord is upon me, because he hath anointed me to preach the gospel to the poor; he hath sent me to heal the brokenhearted , to preach deliverance to the captives, and recovering of sight to the blind, to set at liberty them that are bruised, to preach the acceptable year of the Lord," and then Jesus closes the book, hands the scroll of scripture to the minister, and sits down.

I always found it interesting that after Jesus finished reading, He closed the book. Look at the order here! Jesus wasn't just closing a book because He was finished reading the scripture. Everyone that was in the room understood exactly what was happening. When Jesus closed the book, this was a prophetic action. Jesus was closing the era of Jewish religious rule. Jesus was saying, "Hey, it's a new day!" You can not go into something new until you first close the old. I believe that God is closing a book in your life.

THE JOURNEY

Our life is measured by time. But I like to look at our lives as volumes. Have you ever seen a vast volume of encyclopedias? They are huge! Our lives are not simple days filled with meaningless activities ... Our lives are complex narratives written by the greatest dramaturge ever ... GOD!!! We are not simple people. We have feelings, dreams, aspirations, desires, wills, and agendas. We have a future, a right now, and a past. We have insecurities, insufficiencies, and inadequacies. We are complex beings. We are a limitless library of life experiences, all stacked on a shelf of life, ready to be read of men. Paul said it like this,

Ye are our epistle written in our hearts, known and read of all men (**2 Cor. 3:2**)

Every day of our life is a page. Every major moment is a chapter. Every season is a book, and our lifetime is a volume. GOD IS ABOUT TO CLOSE THE BOOK OF THIS SEASON!!! Jesus told His disciples in Matthew, chapter 16, that the "keys of the kingdom" enabled them to open doors that no man could shut, and CLOSE doors that no man could open. Jesus has closing power. Regardless of what is open in your life right now, GOD HAS THE POWER TO CLOSE IT!

I am Alpha and Omega, the beginning and the end, the first and the last. (**Rev. 22:13**)

Notice the scripture says that Jesus is the "beginning" and the "end". WOW! Jesus is the end. The word "end" is another word for "close." When Jesus shows up, He comes with ending ability. When Jesus shows up, sickness has to end, poverty has to end, drama has to end. JESUS CLOSED THE BOOK! Are you ready for God to open a new book in your life. New adventures, new encounters, fresh winds, and new friends. ARE YOU READY? IT BEGINS NOW!!!

 MEDITATION

Concept: The Integrity of God (**Philippians 1:6**)

What is integrity? Integrity is a concept of consistency of actions, values, methods, measures, principles, expectations, and outcomes. Integrity is meaning what you say, and doing what you decree. Integrity is being consistent in your personality, both in public and in private. Integrity is completing what you start. God doesn't just have integrity, He is integrity because once He speaks it, creation must become what He said. If God thinks it, He becomes it. Our God is integrity. Why is this important? This is important because it allows us to rest assured that what God started in our lives, HE WILL COMPLETE!!!

Today meditate on these questions:
1. What is God starting in my life?
2. What is God ending in my life?
3. If my life was a book, what would be the title?
4. If my life was a movie, would I go see it?
5. If my life was a song, where would it be on the Billboard charts? And what genre would your life be listed in?
6. Would I buy my life if it was available in bookstores, if so, why?
7. What does the ending of your "lifebook" look like?

Scripture Reading:
Isaiah 61, Luke 4:15-22, Isaiah 22:22

ACTIVATION

Today your prophetic exercise is a little bit different. I told you, WE ARE ABOUT TO SHIFT GEARS! Today your prophetic assignment is to go into a bookstore, or go to your library, and choose a book to read for the next 40 days that is NOT a book about ministry. Choose a book on art, science, current events, Christian fiction, or philosophy. Find a book to stretch your thinking. If you are a business owner, get a business book. If you are trying to lose weight, get a book of dieting. Choose a book, in addition to your Bible and ministry material, that you can read and enjoy. Now you may say, "I am already reading something. I have a book I am in right now." Even if you have … CHOOSE A NEW ONE. This is less about reading, and more about the action being mixed with revelation . . . this produces a moment of enlightenment!

Notes

THE JOURNEY

Session Two: Preparation

Day 6

INSPIRATION

Welcome to session two. In Session one we dealt with our past. We looked at behavior patterns, addressed traumatic events, and even accessed revelation to get an understanding of why those events were significant for our development. Today we start a new stream of thought. Session two is all about preparation. You have often heard it said, "failing to plan is planning to fail", this is true. **Most successes and failures happen within the stage of preparation.** Everyone wants success, but the reason the amount of people who are unsuccessful outweigh those who are, is because not everyone is willing to effectively prepare. We have seen people rush into ministry, marriages, and measures, and their lives have never been the same since. Some of you reading this are dealing with situations that are causing you much irritation and frustration because of a lack of preparation.

Here is a principle: The journey must be paid for. Understand that every journey in life must be paid for. Even our entry to Heaven was paid for by Jesus on the cross. You want to walk into the business world? Someone must pay the price for that. You want to have a great marriage? A great marriage must be paid for. Be very careful praying for something you aren't willing to pay for. You will either pay for the journey on the front end, or you will pay for the journey on the back end. You can pay for it in advance by preparation, or you can pay for it later with regret and worry. But either way, YOU MUST PAY THE PRICE!

To prepare means to make ready beforehand for a specific purpose or use. To prepare means to put together or make by combining various elements or ingredients. If you have ever used a recipe to cook, they usually have two durations of time listed: prep time, and cook time. The cook time is how long the food will take to cook and be ready for consumption. But the prep time is how much time the food will take to prepare. How long has it taken God to prepare you? Are you ready for your assignment yet? These are important questions that we must address as we enter purpose. Jesus understood His assignment at 12 years old. Jesus, being found in the temple teaching, said "I must be about my Father's business." After Jesus makes this statement, we don't see Him again until He turns 30 years of age. Jesus had an 18 year preparation period here on the Earth. Did you know that God did NOT start preparing you for your assignment when you received salvation? God has been preparing you the entire way. God uses every circumstance, every mistake, every wrong decision to prepare us for His assignment for our lives.

 MEDITATION

Once you agree upon the price you and your family must pay for success, it enables you to ignore the minor hurts, the opponent's pressure, and the temporary failures.
-Vince Lombardi

When we long for life without difficulties, remind us that oaks grow strong in contrary winds and diamonds are made under pressure.
-Peter Marshall

Preparation comes with pressure. Pressure squeezes a thing into a particular shape or form. Do you feel any pressure? Today's meditation should be coupled with today's activation. Ponder on pressure. What are some pressures you are facing right now? Write them down if you can. Ponder on where the pressure is coming from, and what is the appropriate response. Is this pressure demonic, or is it divine? How long has this amount of pressure been present?

Scripture Reading:
1 Cor. 10:13, John 2:1-11, James 1:12-17

ACTIVATION

Today's activation should be done with today's meditation. Your prophetic assignment today is to write a Haiku. A haiku is a very short and traditional form of Japanese poetry. The poems are very concise, but are packed with significance and meaning. Here are the rules:

1. Only three lines, totaling 17 syllables throughout
2. The first line must be only 5 syllables
3. The second line must be comprised of 7 syllables
4. The third line must be 5 syllables like the first
5. Punctuation and capitalization rules are up to the poet, and need not follow rigid rules used in structuring sentences
6. A haiku does not have to rhyme, in fact many times it does not rhyme at all
7. Some haiku's can include the repetition of words or sounds

Your prophetic assignment is to write a haiku that embodies the emotions and thoughts engendered by the pressure you feel. Take all of your frustration, and limit it to 17 syllables. What you are doing is allowing your pressures to produce creativity. Here's mine:

The world's weight I feel, Worried something may break soon, I was born for this

Day 7

💡 INSPIRATION

Everything in the Kingdom of God is acquired by faith. That may sound simple, but if you've walked with God for any length of time, you understand how difficult this can be. The reason faith can be hard to measure is because faith is both an art and a science. As a science there are laws that govern faith and the actions thereof. But as an art, faith is an ever developing phenomenon used to express an individuals heart for God. Faith is an interesting substance. The word "substance" used in Hebrews, chapter 11 and verse 1, is the Greek word 'hupostasis', and it literally means SUPPORT. The word "faith" literally has less to do with believing, and more to do with location.

Examine yourselves, whether ye be in the faith; prove your own selves. Know ye not your own selves, how that Jesus Christ is in you, except ye be reprobates? (**2 Cor. 13:5**)

Did you read that? Paul said to examine yourselves to see whether you are IN the faith. Faith is a dimension. Faith is a dwelling place. We don't have faith in things, we have faith in a person . . . That person is Jesus. Faith is less about believing and more about location. Where are you planted? What is your current spiritual positioning? Right position produces right perspective. Right perspective produces right image. Right image produces right understanding. Understanding leads to belief, and belief produces behavior. You can never be over-invested in what people say. WATCH WHAT THEY

DO! Faith is NOT just a believing issue, it's a behavior issue. Right believing will always produce right action.

Jesus saith unto him, Thomas, because thou hast seen me, thou hast believed : blessed are they that have not seen , and yet have believed. (**John 20:29**)

You remember Thomas right? Thomas came to be known among the Church as "doubting Thomas", why? Because he made this statement:

The other disciples therefore said unto him, We have seen the Lord. But he said unto them, Except I shall see in his hands the print of the nails, and put my finger into the print of the nails, and thrust my hand into his side, I will not believe. (**John 20:25**)

Notice how Thomas makes a declaration, "I WILL NOT BELIEVE!" Many Believers make the same mistake that Thomas made. Notice that Thomas gives very specific instructions, all of which must happen first, before he believes. Thomas says, "If I am going to believe . . . I have to see his hands, with the nail prints. AND! I must be able to touch it." Have you ever been guilty of that? We are constantly putting synthetic stipulations on our faith, transforming it into an act of our will, not necessarily an act of God. You may be asking, "what does this have to do with preparation?" What is the highest form of faith? PREPARATION. Faith doesn't need evidence to respond . . . Faith is THE EVIDENCE by which I respond. What stipulations have you put on your faith that is delaying your preparation? What are you waiting for to truly step into what God has for your life? What do you feel like you are missing? Whatever you feel like you need . . . guess what? FAITH NEEDS NOTHING BUT A WORD!!! Faith allows you to step out on nothing and say, "LET THERE BE LIGHT!" **Faith allows**

you, even in the uncertainty of life, the foggy mornings of new moments, to step out of the boat of normalcy and walk on the impossible. Faith does not wait for the right time. Faith creates the right time. What I am saying to you is this, a lack of preparation is a sign of a lack of faith. Make no mistake about it, if you believe it's coming . . . YOU WILL PREPARE!!!

MEDITATION

Concept: Faith, as Belief vs. Faith, as Behavior

Faith is both belief and behavior. As a matter of fact, right believing produces right behavior. Today I want you to ponder on the connection between what you believe and what you do. Many times sin is not an issue of blatant rebellion, just misinformation. Take a few minutes and reflect on WHY you do WHAT you do? Here are some questions to consider:

1. Why do I attend the church I go to?
2. Why do I give on the level I give?
3. What am I expecting God to do this week?
4. Do I trust God?
5. Does God trust me?
6. What reasons have I given God to trust me?
7. If my actions reflected my belief, would I be a Believer?

Scripture Reading:
Hebrews 11:1-6, Mark 9:19-29, John 20:20-30

ACTIVATION

This is a unique exercise used to build faith. THIS ACTIVATION TAKES TWO PEOPLE! Two people should be present for this exercise. The two partners can switch after the first one has finished.

THE JOURNEY

You are going to choose a starting point, and a destination (For example: *from your bedroom, to the front door*). Blindfold yourself, and try to make the journey without any help. Use your hands, ears, everything except your eyes, to get to your destination. Now if you are at work, STILL DO IT!!! If someone questions your actions, this is a perfect time to share your faith. During this exercise, TIME YOURSELF and RECORD your time. Then repeat this exercise, but this time, let your partner give you directions. TIME YOURSELF and RECORD your time. Repeat this exercise until your reaction to the word given becomes instantaneous.

Notes

Day 8

💡 INSPIRATION

What is the highest form of faith? PREPARATION. Faith looks like sweat and hard work. You can ask Noah! Noah presents to us a model of faith that is somewhat contradictory to what is being taught in churches today. Faith wasn't for things, cars and clothes ... Faith was used to build. **Faith looked like consistency. Faith looked like repetition. Faith looked like commitment. Faith looked like preparation!** The highest form of faith is preparation! Why? Because faith builds a garage for a car you don't have yet ... Faith builds a family for a legacy you don't have yet ... Faith builds a church for a revival that has not come yet. Faith builds.

Noah was given a promise that it would rain. This word challenged everything about Noah. His understanding of the current world and weather were shattered. I can see Noah grabbing his head while shaking it, screaming "am I going crazy!" Have you ever been there? Faith will make you feel crazy at times, preparing for something you've never seen or experienced. Let's be honest ... Faith is a crazy walk!

But God hath chosen the foolish things of the world to confound the wise; and God hath chosen the weak things of the world to confound the things which are mighty. (1 Cor. 1:27)

To those in the world, faith looks foolish. Why sow a seed when you have bills to pay? Why commit to a movement when you have problems and pressures? Why build a massive boat for a form of precipitation that's never entered the Earth yet? BECAUSE I

BELIEVE!!! I prepare because I believe. I prepare because I expect. I prepare because regardless of what the sky looks like now, I believe RAIN IS COMING!

It is hard for most to prepare, because like Noah, we really don't know what we are preparing for. Most of us live our lives in the ambiguity of vagueness, never realizing the power of specificity. Preparation can only be initiated when a vision or goal has been articulated. When God spoke to Noah about building the Ark of God, He was very specific.

And this is the fashion which thou shalt make it of: The length of the ark shall be three hundred cubits, the breadth of it fifty cubits, and the height of it thirty cubits. A window shalt thou make to the ark, and in a cubit shalt thou finish it above; and the door of the ark shalt thou set in the side thereof; with lower, second, and third stories shalt thou make it. (**Gen. 6:15-16**)

WOW! God even told Moses where to put the doors and the windows. Living in the specificity of God is a great place to be. It is called, HIS PERFECT WILL! It is a place of strength, freedom, and power. God is drawing you into the supernatural life of specificity.

MEDITATION

Concept: The Power of Specific Prayer

God is a God of specifics. When Moses met God in the wilderness, God commanded Moses to build a tabernacle (dwelling place) where God could meet with His people. Moses went up a mountain to commune with God for 40 days. In those 40 days, God gave Moses the Ten Commandments, the Civil and Ceremonial Laws, and also the blueprint for the tabernacle.

According to all that I shew thee, after the pattern of the tabernacle, and the pattern of all the instruments thereof, even so shall ye make it. (**Ex. 25:9**)

God wanted Moses to build the Tabernacle according to HIS directions. Moses couldn't paint it his favorite color. Moses couldn't choose the decor, or even find a location. GOD WAS SPECIFIC. Did you know God has specifics about you? God knows where He wants you to live, and what HE wants you to drive ... God is specific. God desires that we be specific. I have found that the reason many prayers are wasted and spoiled, is because they are prayed amiss. When you pray, BE SPECIFIC! Don't just ask God for healing, call out the name of the disease. BE SPECIFIC! If you want a better house for your family, BE SPECIFIC! How many bedrooms? How many bathrooms? What colors are on the walls, and how many rooms do you want? BE SPECIFIC!!!

Take a few minutes and ponder on the specifics of your need. How much money would you need to be out of debt? What brand of clothes, food, insurance, is your family committed to? What is the name of the street you want to live on? How many square feet is your dream house? What kind of car does your family need? What color is your car? How fast can it go?

Scripture Reading:
James 1, Ex. 25:4-14, 1 Cor. 1:22-31

ACTIVATION

Today we are creating a DESTINY GROCERY LIST! If you could go shopping in the MARKET OF PURPOSE, and everything was free, what would you put in your cart? If you could make a grocery list of all the things you want in life, being VERY specific, what would be on your list?

Notes

DAY 9

💡 INSPIRATION

The anointing is a PREPARED thing. It takes a prepared person to carry the anointing. It is very dangerous to give the anointing to an overnight sensation. A person that has not been prepared won't respect the oil. A person who hasn't survived the process can't appreciate the crushing of the olive. It takes a survivor to appreciate the anointing. While we have been dealing with the power of preparation, it is important to note that God is preparing YOU.

It is not much that takes God by surprise. Our God is omniscient. Omniscient means that God has all knowledge. More accurately omniscient means that God is all knowing. While God is intelligent, it is NOT His brain that gives Him understanding. He IS Wisdom and Truth (**Isa. 11:2, John 14:6**). The scripture says that God declares the end from the beginning (**Isa. 46:10**). What this means is, God is a God of vision. Before God begins a thing, He already has the destination in mind. God never starts a journey, He hasn't completed yet. SELAH! Did you get that? God doesn't start what He can't finish (**Phil. 1:6**). What is preparation? Preparation is the middle part. Between the beginning and the end of a thing, there is a great chasm called preparation. Between your dream and its fulfillment, there is a gap called preparation that many have perished trying to cross. Preparation separates the men from the boys and the women from the girls. Preparation is the filter by which phonies are found out. Preparation is the process of turning vision into reality. Preparation is the middle part. Let's be honest! It's easy to shout when you receive the prophecy. It's even easier to celebrate when you see the fulfillment of the promise. But the true test of faith is, can you rejoice when God is breaking you. Can you smile when God is ripping your life apart? Like a Tornado, He is trashing all your plans and destroying all your cute baby names, throwing all your degrees and diplomas out the window. Can you smile then? GOD WILL INTERRUPT YOUR LIFE! It is hard to smile during the middle part.

When you look at the process that the anointing oil goes through, it is quite fascinating. There are five ingredients to the anointing: myrrh, cinnamon, cane or calamus, cassia, and oil from an olive.

Also take for yourself quality spices--five hundred shekels of liquid myrrh, half as much sweet-smelling cinnamon (two hundred and fifty shekels), two hundred and fifty shekels of sweet-smelling cane, five hundred shekels of cassia, according to the shekel of the sanctuary, and a hin of olive oil. And you shall make from these a holy anointing oil. (**Exodus 30:23-25**)

Each one of these ingredients have their own purpose. Alone and independent from each other, they still have value and significance. But something supernatural happens when you begin to mix these components together. Something chemical happens when all of these separate parts come together to create a new substance. I wish I had time to tell you that this is actually the mystery of the local church. We don't have time, trust me!

God takes all the individual parts, pieces, and points of our life and He uses them, like a Master Chef, to prepare the greatest meal of our life, DESTINY! I hope you're hungry.

MEDITATION

Concept: The Anointing (**Ex. 30:23-25, Isa. 10:27**)

The Anointing is God's enabling power. To be anointed means to be empowered by the spirit. The anointing is God empowering an individual to complete a task. The anointing enables man to perform like God. There is man speed, and then there is God speed. The anointing, resting on man, enables man to access the speed limit of God, and accomplish assignments by acceleration.

Take a moment and ponder on some odds that you have overcome. I know you may think that it was will power, or even emotional strength. What if it was really the anointing that saved you? What if it was the anointing that got you through the divorce? What if it was the anointing that stopped the overdose? What if it was the anointing that kept you alive in the car accident? The anointing is NOT just for preaching. The anointing is for SURVIVAL! What have you survived? Think about it, AND THANK GOD!!!

Scripture Reading:
Ex. 30:23-25, Luke 4:18-19, 2 Cor. 11:20-30

ACTIVATION

Are they ministers of Christ? (I speak as a fool) I am more; in labours more abundant, in stripes above measure, in prisons more frequent, in deaths oft. Of the Jews five times received I forty stripes save one. Thrice was I beaten with rods , once was I stoned , thrice I suffered shipwreck , a night and a day I have been in the deep; In journeyings often, in perils of waters, in perils of robbers, in perils by mine own countrymen, in perils by the heathen, in perils in the city, in perils in the wilderness, in perils in the sea, in perils among false brethren; In weariness and painfulness, in watchings often, in hunger and thirst, in fastings often, in cold and nakedness. Beside those things that are without, that which cometh upon me daily, the care of all the churches. (**2 Cor. 11:23-28**)

Paul gives us a list of all of his hardships. Paul was very vocal about his failures and fights. Yesterday, we went grocery shopping, but today we are about to prepare a meal. But first, we need a recipe. Today your assignment is to write down all of the HARDSHIPS you have been through (choose major moments), and write them down as a recipe. Be as blunt and real as possible. Record candidly about your failures and bad decisions. Let's see what God is cooking!

Notes

Day 10

💡 INSPIRATION

The Word of God is released on levels. Every word is NOT the same. There are SIX LEVELS of the Word of God. Let's go through these quickly:

1. **Water-** Eph. 5:26 speaks of the washing of water by the word of God. When we are first born again, we must be washed. Just like a new born baby coming into the world must be washed, so do we require washing as we enter the Kingdom of God.
2. **Milk-** Milk is for babies. These are the fundamental and foundational truths of scripture. This is used to build the skeletal system, or the foundation of the Believer's faith (**1 Peter 2:2**)
3. **Bread-** Jesus said that men should not live by bread alone, not by no bread at all. Bread represents doctrine. Bread represents law. Bread represents revelation that can be given in bites (crumbs), waves (slices), and downloads (loaves). (**Matt. 4:4**)
4. **Meat-** The book of Hebrews speaks about strong meat. Meat is the diet of sons. Luke 15 says that when the son was restored, the father killed and served a fatted calf. MEAT! Meat is for those who have developed teeth. Meat is for those looking for more than a prophecy ... they are looking for destiny. Meat must be chewed and digested (**Heb. 5:12,14**)
5. **Mystery-** In Matthew 13, Jesus speaks to His disciples about mysteries. Paul said that we were stewards of the mysteries of God. A mystery is revelation that God hides in darkness.

There are certain truths that God must hide, they are called dark sayings because God hides them in thick darkness. Moses accessed this level of revelation (**Ex. 20:21**).
6. **Corn-** Corn is the diet of apostles. In Mark 2:23-25, the apostles are found picking "heads" of corn. A head of corn represents generations, rank, and headship. Every office and gift needs a diet that matches its rank to be sustained. Corn represents the power to produce another generation. Apostles are fathers that are dedicated to raising generations, not just ministries and measures.

What level of the Word of God do you eat on a regular basis? What level of the Word of God is released in your local church on a regular basis? Are you eating according to your rank? Can you survive off of leftovers? **Every office and gift needs a diet that matches its rank to be sustained**. Today we conclude session two, the topic of preparation. Are you prepared for your assignment? Have you been adequately trained to wield the Word of God with accuracy and power?

Every journey in life must be prepared for. Jesus said, "For which of you, intending to build a tower, sitteth not down first, and counteth the cost, whether he have sufficient to finish it" (**Luke 14:28**). Never start a journey you can't finish. Never make a promise you can't deliver. Never pray a prayer, you are not willing to pay the price for. Never ask a question, if the answer will break you. You must be willing to count the cost if you are going to complete the journey. Have you prepared for the journey?

And as he lay and slept under a juniper tree, behold, then an angel touched him, and said unto him, Arise and eat . 6 And he looked , and, behold, there was a cake baken on the coals, and a cruse of water at his head. And he did eat and drink , and laid him down again . 7 And the angel of the LORD came again the second time, and touched him, and said , Arise and eat ; because the journey is too great for thee. (**1 Kings 19:5-7**)

Notice that verse 7 says "arise and eat, for the journey is too great for thee." We are all on a journey. While our journeys are tailor made to fit our purpose, they are all filled with different pressures and pains. This is why we can't be jealous of people. Honestly, you should never be envious of another person's gift or anointing, because you don't know what their journey required of them. Some people have lost family members, some have lost marriages, others have lost sanity, but we have all paid a price. Elijah at this point in his life and ministry feels like giving up . . . He is on "E". His gas tank of enthusiasm and motivation is "empty". Have you ever been there? Elijah actually begs God to kill him. HE CONSIDERS SUICIDE! But it's because he has not been eating right. Whenever your spiritual diet is lacking balance, your emotional dimension usually reacts with turbulence. This can feel like depression, anxiety, and even fear and frustration.

Every journey requires a diet. Have you ever went on a long road trip just to be detoured or delayed because someone didn't use the bathroom? **When people do not prepare effectively, destinies are delayed.** Have you taken the time to eat for your journey? Are you planted in a good local church where you can be taught the scripture? Are you being washed by the word of God consistently? Great journeys require great diets. Great people require great preparation. Elijah's ministry demanded that he eat on another level. His appetite had to shift, His palate had to be upgraded, His diet had to go to the next level! ARE YOU READY FOR A DIET CHANGE?

MEDITATION

Concept: The Mysteries of God (**1 Cor. 2:7**)

It is the glory of God to conceal a thing: but the honour of kings is to search out a matter. (**Prov. 25:2**)

God loves hiding things, just to find out who really wants His heart. Today I want you to ponder on the mysteries of God. Instead of a scripture reading, take a moment and open your Bible and look at the different mysteries of scripture. These mysteries listed below are some deep truths of scripture that should be explored. TAKE A MOMENT AND DO THIS NOW!

1. Mystery of The Fullness of the times of the Gentiles. **Rom. 8:10**
2. Mystery of The Indwelling of the Holy Spirit. **1 Cor. 2:6-16**
3. Mystery of God's Will **Eph. 1:9**
4. Mystery of The dispensation of Grace. **Eph. 3:3**
5. Mystery of The fellowship of believers. **Eph. 3:9**
6. Mystery of The church as the Bride of Christ. **Eph. 5:32**
7. Mystery of the Gospel. **Eph. 6:19**
8. Mystery of Christ. **Col. 4:3**
9. Mystery of Iniquity **II Thess. 2:7**
10. Mystery of Faith **Luke 17:7-9**
11. Mystery of Godliness **I Tim. 3:16**
12. Mystery of Seven Churches of Asia **Rev. 1:20**
13. Mystery of Babylon **Rev. 17:5,7**

ACTIVATION

Today your Prophetic Assignment is to BUY LUNCH FOR SOMEONE! We are all on a journey and require nourishment. Today while you are at work, or out and about, do a RANDOM ACT OF KINDNESS, and BUY SOMEONE LUNCH. It doesn't have to be expensive, just be prayerful. Get someone a sandwich, a burger, or a salad. I promise you, your gift is about to kick in.

Notes

Session Three: Potential

Day 11

💡 INSPIRATION

What is your limitations? How much can you take? What is your tipping point? We all have a breaking point, you know, the point of no return. We all have thresholds. A threshold is a limitation. Have you ever heard of the term, 'pain threshold'? Your pain threshold is the amount of pain you can take before breaking down. Your intelligence threshold is the amount of information you can receive before you brain begins to regurgitate the data. We all have limitations? What are your emotional limitations? How much heartache can you take? How much betrayal can you take? How many lies can people tell on your before you quit? Your limitations are important because the enemy will use them to exploit your weaknesses. Your limitations determine how the enemy responds to you. Your limitations determine the assignment God gives you. Your limitations determine how far you will go in life. People with a low pain threshold usually don't go very far in life, because all good things are guarded by pain. Pain filters out those who just "want" success from those who actually "need" to succeed. Pain reveals motive. Pain exposes hearts. Pain will make you tell the truth even when you want to lie. It's pain!

Your limitations tell a lot about you. Whether you want to believe or not, your limitations can be eliminated. Your weaknesses can be addressed, and the boundaries of your potential can be enlarged. Over the next five days, we will be strategically postured to pull and stretch the muscles of your potential. WE JUST SHIFTED GEARS.

For the kingdom of heaven is as a man travelling into a far country, who called his own servants, and delivered unto them his goods. 15 And unto one he gave five talents, to another two, and to another one; to every man according to his several ability; and straightway took his journey. (**Matthew 25:14-15**)

This is a very familiar passage of scripture. Notice that it begins by saying, "for the kingdom of heaven is as …", this means that the kingdom of God is being compared and/or explained through a parable. A parable is when a spiritual model is compared with a physical model for the purpose of articulation. A parable is when a spiritual truth is explained in a natural way for the purpose of clarification. Jesus would use parables to teach people spiritual truths. Jesus shows us here that the Kingdom of God operates in a certain way. The Kingdom of God is a reward system. God never gives us what we pray for, He only gives us what we can handle. This is the Law of Capacity.

There hath no temptation taken you but such as is common to man: but God is faithful, who will not suffer you to be tempted above that ye are able; but will with the temptation also make a way to escape, that ye may be able to bear it. (**1 Cor. 10:13**)

God knows your breaking point! God knows your limitations! Regardless of what you're facing right now, IT WON'T BREAK YOU! God is stretching the limitations of your potential. I know it hurts, and I know it is uncomfortable, but God is making you better. Better hurts. We often speak about trusting God, but rarely realize the fact that God trusts us with trouble. The talents that God gave the servants in Matthew 25 were responsibility. Some say that they each received a few thousand dollars. What they were given is less important than what they did with what they were given. These talents could have been problems that needed solutions. These talents could have been relationships that needed navigation. These talents could have been opportunities and open doors. Regardless of what the talents were, they were given according to potential.

MEDITATION
Concept: The Law of Capacity (**Matthew 25:14-25**)

The Law of Capacity states that you don't get what you pray for, you get what you can manage. You could pray for money, but if your limitation is a thousand dollars, you will never be given more than that. God wants to bless you, but He doesn't want to break you. Every blessing has weight, and every Believer has a limit. Once the blessing exceeds your limit, it turns into a curse. Have you ever been broken by what should have been a blessing?

Today I want you to meditate on your limitations. You may want to take notes during this exercise. Ponder on your thresholds, these in particular:

1. What is your submission limit? How much correction, direction, and instruction can you take before pride is seen?
2. What is your emotional threshold? How much emotion, whether it be romance or tragedy, can you take before the tears begin to flow? Some of us cry during sad movies, others aren't distracted at the most graphic scenes.
3. What is your pain threshold? How much pain can you take? When have you ever given up because of pain? Can you remember a situation that made you quit?
4. What is your financial threshold? How much can you give before you choke? How much money can be required of you before your bills are neglected? How much money can you receive before you start acting "brand new"?

5. What is your spiritual threshold? How much church can you take before your attention begins to wander? How long can you pray? How much mentorship do you want?

Understand that the boundaries of your limitations can be moved. You are responsible for challenging your potential. Take a moment and ponder your limitations in these areas. Your strength in these areas will determine what God can give you, what doors are opened for you, and how far you go in life. You can not use the excuse, "I CAN'T TAKE IT", God is requiring you to address your tipping point, and **SHIFT YOUR LIMITATIONS**.

Scripture Reading:
Jonah 1:6-17, 2:1-6, Ephesians 3:15-21, Genesis 1:6-16

ACTIVATION

Today's prophetic exercise is designed to test a few of your limitations. Each one of these exercises can be repeated to get better results, and to increase your capacity.

EMOTIONAL THRESHOLD: Is there something you went through that is hard to speak about. Your emotional threshold grows with transparency and accountability. The more you tell the story, the easier it becomes to face the reality of the situation. Communication helps strengthen the emotional realm of a person. Find a friend, and have a HARD CONVERSATION. Is there someone you need to apologize to, or forgive. Today, have a HARD CONVERSATION, and see where your emotions begin to surface. Remember, this is less about the conversation, and more about you gaging when your emotions kick in.

SUBMISSION (SERVICE) THRESHOLD: Find a way to volunteer MORE TIME at your local church. How long can you serve before you need a break? This is important! How can you pray, "Lord send me to nations", if you can't serve without complaining in your local church. Are you active in your local assembly? What ministries do you serve in? Volunteer at your local church, but volunteer for something that is not glamorous. Clean the bathrooms, mop the floor, or serve the homeless.

Depending on your church, this may or may not be feasible. If this is not, pick a room in your house to clean, and repeat this exercise until you get distracted and uninterested.

ATTENTION THRESHOLD: Find a book, and start reading. TIME YOURSELF. Continue reading until your attention begins to wander. You can also do this exercise with a television show or music playlist. This can be tricky, because most forms of entertainment are created to captivate your attention, so this exercise must be done intentionally. You are looking for the breaking of your concentration. Once the cords of your concentration begin to break, this is revealing that you've reached your limitation.

Notes

Day 12

💡 INSPIRATION

Have you ever surprised yourself by something you did? Have you ever shocked yourself by your own actions? Many times when faced with significant challenges, a different dimension of ourselves emerges, and another man is born! Has this ever happened to you? It happened to Saul! In 1 Samuel, chapter 10, after Saul has misplaced his donkey, he finds himself in a company of prophets.

After that thou shalt come to the hill of God, where is the garrison of the Philistines: and it shall come to pass, when thou art come thither to the city, that thou shalt meet a company of prophets coming down from the high place with a psaltery, and a tabret, and a pipe, and a harp, before them; and they shall prophesy : 6 And the Spirit of the LORD will come upon thee, and thou shalt prophesy with them, and shalt be turned into another man. (**1 Sam. 10:5-6**)

Notice that verse 6 says that Saul will be "turned" into another man. Saul had prophetic potential, but it wasn't released until he was in the right company. Our company has a lot to do with what is pulled out of us. The people around us affect our potential.

I am often surprised when I hear people say what they will "never" do. One thing that life has taught me is that you should never underestimate your potential, for good or bad. Life will challenge you. Life will stretch you. Life will manipulate moments that pull out the worse in you. And likewise, life has a way, in the darkest of moments, to allow beauty to shine forth. The truth is, most of us have no idea what is in us. It takes living a while to realize that you are not as pretty as you thought you were. It takes going through life to realize that the storm couldn't kill you. Saul was just looking for a donkey, and now he meets destiny. He didn't know he had prophetic power, but he stepped in the right place at the right time. It takes the right people, and the right places, to activate the potential inside of us. Paul said,

Wherefore I put thee in remembrance that thou stir up the gift of God, which is in thee by the putting on of my hands. (**2 Tim. 1:6**)

Paul was speaking to Timothy about potential. Potential is possibility. Possibilities are activated by problems. Problems reveal our potential. That's why God will put your, "I WILL NEVER", to the test. God wants to stretch you until you feel like you are going to break, just for you to realize that breaking isn't in you. Potential must be discovered. You can ask Peter! You never know that you can walk on water, until there is a storm that forces you out of the boat. You didn't know you could take care of the family alone, until you had no choice. You didn't know you could work two jobs until you got the eviction notice. You never knew you could withstand this type of tragedy, but LOOK AT YOU!!! You are still here. It takes a problem to reveal the depth of our potential. **Problems are not our enemy. Problems are the platform on which our potential performs.** I have heard stories of petite mothers lifting cars off of their baby, because you don't know what's in you, until you're faced with an impossibility. You want to know what's in you, FIND A PROBLEM!!!

MEDITATION

Concept: The Longsuffering of the Lord (**Psalm 86:15**)

When we begin to address the character of God, there are a few things that come to mind. God is patient, kind, gracious, merciful, consistent, trustworthy, and so much more. But one of His characteristics that continually blows my mind is His longsuffering. Longsuffering is defined as endurance. Longsuffering is defined as having or showing patience in spite of troubles, especially those caused by other people. God can handle your hang ups. God is interested in your development, not your demise. God is not trying to punish you, but pull out your potential.

Take a moment and ponder on the longsuffering of the Lord. How much has God endured from you? In truth God should have walked away from us a long time ago, but He has made a commitment to never leave us or forsake us (**Hebrews 13:5**). Take a few minutes and thank the Lord audibly (out loud). When was the last time you gave God a commanded praise? Right now, drop everything you are doing, and begin to praise the Lord … GO!

Scripture Reading:
1 Samuel 10, Hebrews 13:1-10, Psalm 86

ACTIVATION

Today is a test of your patience and endurance. Your prophetic exercise today is silence. Silence releases the power of reflection. Now this may stretch you. Choose an hour to dedicate to the Lord today. Once you have chosen your time, I want you to find a quiet place and spend time with the Lord, but this is the trick, YOU CAN NOT SAY A WORD. This is NOT prayer time, it is reflection time. Take ONE HOUR to just rest in His presence. HE IS GOING TO TALK TO YOU! For ONE HOUR, don't say anything, just write down everything you hear!

Day 13

💡 INSPIRATION

Potential is a muscle you can stretch by challenging your limitations. Great people understand that you only become great by pushing yourself to your limits. Limits, we all have them. We all have a "last nerve" that we are praying no one touches. We all have our "hulk" moments where we allow our emotions to take over. We all have limits. Potential is the sum total of what you can manage. How much can you take before you scream "I quit!" This is very important, because whatever your limitation is, the devil is going to push you to that place. This is not the moment to make excuses, nor the time to whine. STRETCH YOURSELF!

And in the fourth watch of the night Jesus went unto them, walking on the sea. 26 And when the disciples saw him walking on the sea, they were troubled, saying, It is a spirit; and they cried out for fear. 27 But straightway Jesus spake unto them, saying, Be of good cheer; it is I; be not afraid. 28 And Peter answered him and said, Lord, if it be thou, bid me come unto thee on the water. 29 And he said, Come. And when Peter was come down out of the ship, he walked on the water, to go to Jesus. (**Matt. 14:25-29**)

It was the fourth watch. In our darkest moments God is still working destiny. The fourth watch represented the darkest part of the night. The fourth watch had to be taken by the fisherman who had the greatest eyes. The fourth watch was for the fearless. Peter took this watch. Peter was one of those people that answered the question before it was completely asked. Peter was impulsive, and always trying to impress his peers. Peter wanted you to know his potential. And even with all of Peter's testosterone, the scripture says that he was afraid. Notice that Jesus didn't appear during the sunny moments of this journey . . . Jesus showed up during the fourth watch!

And the people stood afar off, and Moses drew near unto the thick darkness where God was. (**Ex. 20:21**)

WOW! Did you read that? God was found in thick darkness. Potential grows as you address limitations, admit weaknesses, and face your fears. What is fear? Fear is an emotion that usually produces paralysis. Fear stops people in their tracks. Have you ever been home alone just to hear an unidentified sound? What did you do? **Fear incarcerates you to the present moment, never allowing you to see the reward of conquering the challenge.** Fear makes cowards out of conquerors.

For God hath not given us the spirit of fear; but of power, and of love, and of a sound mind. (**2 Tim. 1:7**)

Fear doesn't come from God. Fear is the feeling produced when we are taken out of our comfort zone. This is what storms do for us. God creates storms to take us out of our comfort zone, so that the depths of our potential is revealed. This happens to us all. This also happened to Peter. Peter is on a boat surrounded by his friends, a place of comfort and control. Comfort is the enemy to greatness. Comfort makes greatness look free, but trust me, it is an illusion. We all come to a point where we must face our fears. What are your fears? What is your phobia? Whatever you are afraid of, you can not go further than. Whatever you are afraid of, you are bound to. Whatever you are afraid of, is what you must defeat to become great. Your potential grows as you intentionally challenge your limitations.

Do you have stage fright? Greatness for you is on the stage. Are you afraid of crowds? Your deliverance is among people!
Peter put pressure on his potential, and it made him bigger than the boat he was in. Society will put us in boats. Even family members can sometimes limit us. People may limit you to your past, your proclivities, or even your pocket book, but REPEAT THIS AFTER ME: I AM MORE THAN WHAT YOU SEE (repeat 7 times aloud). Today, intentionally challenge your fears, your limitations, and your comfort zone!

MEDITATION

Concept: Boldness of the Believer (**Acts 1:8, 4:13**)

Boldness is defined as the trait of being willing to undertake things that involve risk or danger. Boldness is produced by confidence. Fear attacks your confidence by moving you into the realm of the "unknown". God gives us faith to navigate through the darkness. No matter how much fear the fourth watch wants to force on you, you must be bold.

Let us therefore come boldly unto the throne of grace, that we may obtain mercy, and find grace to help in time of need. (**Hebrews 4:16**)

What gives us boldness? BLOOD! The writer of Hebrews says that we should come "boldly" unto the throne of grace . . . Blood gives us the confidence of approach. Jesus, when He died on the cross, conquered any and every devil that could cause fear. YOU HAVE NOTHING TO FEAR! What would you try, if you had no fear? What would you do, where would you go, who would you minister to if you had no fear? Take a moment to ponder about opportunities you've lost because of fear. Here are some questions to consider:

1. What are my fears?
2. What situations did I not fully enjoy because of fear?
3. How many opportunities did I squander because of fear?
4. I am very uncomfortable when . . . ?
5. My greatest fear is . . . ?
6. When am I most nervous?
7. How long will I be afraid?

Scripture Reading:
Hebrews 4:11-16, Mark 9:19-29, Acts 1:1-8

ACTIVATION

Today your prophetic exercise is to diagnose and FACE YOUR FEAR!!! Today your assignment is to document your fear, and then record what happens when you address it. This may take several tries, and even may be an exercise you must do on a daily basis to build boldness. You must constantly address your fears to build your potential. What is your fear? What must you do to conquer it?

Notes

Day 14

💡 INSPIRATION

In order for potential to shift into power, it must be discovered, defined, and developed. Training pulls out potential. Every stage of our life has potential. As a single, there is potential. As a husband, there is potential. Most people just rush through life, never truly maximizing the potential of the moment they are in. **People who are serious about tapping their potential understand the power of investment**. There is a difference between saving and investing. Saving has nothing to do with potential. When you save a dollar, you are limiting the dollar to its face value. But investing is all about potential. Investing is being able to see beyond face value, and peering into one's potential.

I thank God for the people who have invested in me throughout the years. If it wasn't for someone seeing something special in me, I wouldn't be where I am now. It is great when someone can see the gift of God on your life. But if it's anyone who should be able to see your worth, it should be you. How much do you invest in yourself? The only reason people do not invest in themselves, is because they don't know their potential. Potential is pulled out by training and mentorship. We see this in the life of the disciples.

And he saith unto them, Follow me, and I will make you fishers of men. (**Matthew 4:19**)

The majority of the disciples were fishermen. These men had been trained since childhood on how to catch, clean, and cook fish. They were skilled at fishing. Most of the disciples had dedicated their entire lives to fishing. And when Jesus comes, He shifts their development. Everything they have been through, all the training they have acquired, Jesus is now going to reveal the true purpose of their process. "Follow me, and I will make you fishers of men." Jesus spent three years investing in these men, pulling out their potential. Let's look at how intense their training was.

In Luke, chapter 24, after Jesus has been crucified and buried, we are met by two men on a road to Emmaus. These two men are speaking with each other concerning the scripture, and all of a sudden Jesus shows up. Now Jesus walks with them for 7 miles (which is a day's journey), and in that time He explicates the entirety of the scripture. In a day's journey, Jesus unlocks the scripture for them, from Genesis to Malachi, explaining all things pertaining to Himself. Now Jewish teachers believed that it took a lifetime to come to this level of knowledge. A lifetime is about 60 to 70 years. I want you to understand the level of investment the disciples received. Now if these men on the road to Emmaus received this level of education in one day, what type of education did the disciples receive if they walked with Jesus everyday, for three years?

LET'S THINK ABOUT THIS: If the men on the road to Emmaus received 60 years of teaching in a day's journey, let us see the level of education the disciples had. So if the disciples were with Jesus for 3 1/2 years, which is 42 months, which equates to 1260 days. If one day equals a lifetime of learning, the disciples received 75,600 years of training. In just over 3 1/2 years, Jesus gave them 75,600 years worth of education. Now that is investment.

If you believe that you are more than you are right now, you would invest in yourself. If you truly believed in your future, in your gift, in the assignment of God on your life, you would invest in it. Tapping potential is all about investment. You must be willing to invest in the right training, the right reading, the right friends, the right atmosphere, and the right leadership if you are truly interested in becoming all that God has called you to be. Potential must move from acknowledgment to actuality, this is done through training. How much training have you received in your assignment? What is your current level of submission? Do you have a pastor? What church are you planted in? Are you actively involved at your local church?

MEDITATION

"Focusing your life solely on making a buck shows a certain poverty of ambition. It asks too little of yourself. Because it's only when you hitch your wagon to something larger than yourself that you realize your true potential." -*Barack Obama*

"Ever since I was a child I have had this instinctive urge for expansion and growth. To me, the function and duty of a quality human being is the sincere and honest development of one's potential."
-*Bruce Lee*

"If you are against yourself, you will never reach your highest potential. And when you criticize yourself, you're criticizing God."
- *Joel Osteen*

"Everyone has inside of themselves a piece of good news. The good news is that you don't know how great you can be! How much you can love! What you can accomplish! And what your potential is!"
-*Anne Frank*

These four quotes are from people with very different backgrounds, paths, and journeys in life. Take a moment a ponder on each of these quotes, while asking yourself these questions:
1. What am I doing to invest in my potential?
2. Where is the majority of my finances going?
3. How much do I spend on my own development and training?
4. Am I investing in the right leadership?
5. Am I investing in those around me?
6. If my level of investment revealed my level of faith, where would my faith be?
7. What skills should I be investing in?

Scripture Reading:
Luke 24:13-31, Matthew 4:14-24, Judges 6:14

ACTIVATION

WE ARE ABOUT TO SHIFT GEARS!!! Today your job is to invest in yourself. This will be like a spiritual scavenger hunt. **THIS EXERCISE WILL TAKE MONEY.** If you are afraid to spend money to invest in yourself, your potential is decaying already. Don't be cheap when it comes to destiny. Get a new pen, make it a nice one. If you already have an unused one in your house, utilize that one. Assign this pen to this assignment.

Day 15

💡 INSPIRATION

Who's hand are you under? Every great masterpiece was made at the hand of a great artist. Whether it's Michelangelo's Pieta, Da Vinci's Mona Lisa, Rachmaninoff's Prelude in G Minor, or even Dwayne Wade's Eurostep, every masterpiece is made at the hands of a master. While the masterpiece went through a process of creation, and while people will line up and pay big money to see these works of art, we can never take for granted the process the artist went through. Every artist is at some point a work of art.

Jeremiah was commanded by God to go down to the potter's house, and there God was going to show him a parable. When Jeremiah arrives, he sees a potter shaping and molding an awkward piece of clay. The artist in frustration, seeing the piece of clay not taking shape, patiently starts the process over. The artist does not give up on the project, for the artist understands that if the jar is hurt in the making, it can still be changed and be made right by the potter, for the clay is still soft. God showed Jeremiah this vision to reassure Jeremiah that God is the Great Picasso, and any mistake He can turn into a masterpiece. This vision fortified God's covenant with Israel and gave Israel hope for the future.

Every great masterpiece is made under the hand of a great artist. We see this is Genesis, chapter 2. In Genesis chapter 2, we get a chance to glance over God's shoulder as He is at the potter's wheel creating a masterpiece. This masterpiece is called Man.

And the LORD God formed man of the dust of the ground, and breathed into his nostrils the breath of life; and man became a living soul. (**Gen. 2:7**)

The word "form" in the Hebrew literally means to squeeze, or to apply pressure. When God showed Jeremiah the vision of the potter, He was actually showing Jeremiah how He created mankind. Adam, with all of his failures and frailties, was still a prized possession. In 1948, Jackson Pollock officially sold his painting, entitled No. 5, for approximately 162 million dollars. Now if you see this piece of art, it doesn't look like much. When you view No. 5, it looks like something any of us could do. I asked God why did this painting cost so much, and God said to me, "it's because whose hand touched it!" Regardless of your imperfections, you still have value because of the artist who made you. If a Picasso could go for millions, what are you worth. The same artist that made you also created the stars and the Sun. We are in great company!

Joshua understood the pressure of being under the hand of a great artist. Joshua was the spiritual son of Moses. Joshua had submitted his life under the hand of Moses.

And Joshua the son of Nun was full of the spirit of wisdom; for Moses had laid his hands upon him: and the children of Israel hearkened unto him, and did as the LORD commanded Moses. (**Deut. 34:9**)

Joshua understood the power of submission. Joshua submitted his entire life to his pastor, mentor, and spiritual father. Joshua, like the clay on the potter's wheel, allowed Moses to make him into a masterpiece. Dirt has no innate value. Dirt is not expensive, on the contrary, dirt is cheap. Have you ever heard the expression, "cheap as dirt?" But our God is able to take cheap things, and turn them into paintings that sell for 162 million dollars. Who's hand are you under? Who are you allowing to shape your life? Paternal power, and spiritual leadership is the key to pulling out our potential. God commits us into the hands of great artist, hoping that we surrender our will, so we can be shaped into something great. This is not a fun place to be in . . . it is a hard place to dwell. Being under the hand of a great artist, you are always surrounded by pressure, breaking, and cycles. There is nothing compared to the python-like pressure of paternal power. You need someone to break you! You need someone who will commit their life to seeing you shaped for destiny. As the artist applies pressure, his very identity (fingerprints) is imprinted into our very being. As we conclude session three, let's focus on honoring those who pour into our lives and work diligently to make us masterpieces.

MEDITATION

Concept: Headship (**Psalm 133:2**)

Headship is an apostolic concept on order, government, rank, and function. When Adam was created, he was the "head" of humanity. Adam was the General of the Human race. The word "head" denotes leadership, direction, and the highest rank of a thing. Headship is a governmental term denoting set leadership and power. The husband is the "head" of the house. The Senior Pastor is the "head" of the local church. Jesus Christ is the "head" of the Body of Christ.

But I would have you know , that the head of every man is Christ; and the head of the woman is the man; and the head of Christ is God. (**1 Cor. 11:3**)

Headship symbolizes the place where vision originates, for this is where the eyes are. Headship symbolizes the place where commands are released, for this is where the mouth is. The "head" always receives the anointing first, and then the beard (leadership) and the skirt (fellowship). Take a moment and ponder on the leadership in your life, and where you are now as a result of being on the potter's wheel. Here are some questions to consider:

1. Who am I 'really' submitted to?
2. Who does God have shaping my life?
3. If I was a piece of art, what kind would I be? (For ex. song, painting, sculpture, etc?)
4. If I was a piece of art, what would my name be?
5. What is my level of loyalty, submission, and dedication to the leadership I am under?
6. How am I serving my local church?
7. How can I show extravagant honor to the leadership in my life?

ACTIVATION

Art is more than self expression, it is therapeutic. Many people paint, sculpt, build, or create music to relax and release tension. Today's prophetic exercise is to create a masterpiece! YES YOU! Create a drawing, painting, song, poem, or any piece of art that expresses your gratitude and honor towards the leadership in your life.

Notes

_____
_____
_____
_____
_____

Session Four: Purpose

THE JOURNEY

Day 16

💡 INSPIRATION

Today we begin day one of session four. We are almost halfway finished. This is not the moment to slack off, but to lean in with all of your weight. WE JUST SHIFTED GEARS!!! Purpose. We have all been more than acquainted with this word and concept. Most Christians are very familiar with purpose. We understand that we were created, we were made, we were formed for a purpose. Everything that God creates has purpose. We see what God created in the very first verse of scripture:

In the beginning God created the heaven and the earth. (**Gen. 1:1**)

The word for "God" here is the word *Elohim*. Elohim is one of the many names of God, and denotes His function, power, and authority as creator. God is a master creator. It is important that we establish in our theology that everything God creates has a purpose. Purpose is significant because purpose reveals function. When you don't know the purpose of a thing, abuse is inevitable. If you don't know the purpose of a person, you can make a lifelong commitment to someone that God only intends to be around for a season. When you don't know the purpose of a thing, you can never utilize it correctly. Many of us have been abusing people, ministries, and even money, because we don't understand their purpose.

Genesis is known as the book of beginnings. There is a hermeneutic law, called the principle of first mention, that says if you want to know God's intent for a thing, you must find when it was first established or first mentioned. It is in Genesis that the precedent of

God is set. Genesis is a legal book that sets the standard for all other proceeding scripture. So it only makes sense, if we are trying to discover purpose, that we go back to the beginning.

And the earth was without form, and void; and darkness was upon the face of the deep. And the Spirit of God moved upon the face of the waters. 3 And God said, Let there be light: and there was light. 4 And God saw the light, that it was good: and God divided the light from the darkness. 5 And God called the light Day, and the darkness he called Night. And the evening and the morning were the first day. (**Gen. 1:2-5**)

God begins the creative process. For seven days, God not only creates "things", but He establishes systems. Every day God is going to establish a self sustaining system.

7 Creational Days- *7 Creational Systems*
1. Greater Light and Lesser Light
2. Sky and Sea
3. Land and Vegetation
4. Sun, Moon and Stars
5. Fish and Birds
6. Man and Beast
7. Sabbath

On the first day God creates light or revelation. You can not build anything without revelation. Light is needed to work. Jesus said this,

I must work the works of him that sent me, while it is day: the night cometh, when no man can work. (**John 9:4**)

When people do not have revelation, they waste time working without an understanding of purpose. Work, minus purpose, equals slavery. You must have revelation of purpose! You must know why you do what you do! Purpose is the WHAT and WHY of your calling from God. In this session, get ready to discover the WHAT and WHY of your existence. WE JUST SHIFTED GEARS!!!

MEDITATION

"He who has a why to live for can bear almost any how."
-Friedrich Nietzsche

"It is not enough to be industrious; so are the ants. What are you industrious about?"
-Henry David Thoreau

Today, ponder on purpose. Questions are the gateways to answers. There are a few questions that I want you to meditate on today. We are going to do something a tad different. Today we are going to meditate aloud. Meditation is a form of mental repetition, done for the purpose of recalibrating the way our mind processes information. Find a quiet place and repeat these questions aloud as many times as you can, writing everything that comes to mind as you are doing this. Here are some questions to ponder:

1. Why am I here?
2. What is my purpose?
3. What do I want my legacy to be when I leave this planet?
4. Am I needed in this time?
5. How am I going to make an impact on my Generation?
6. Am I a leader?
7. If I only had ONE YEAR to live, what would I spend my time doing?
8. Am I committed to something bigger than me?

Scripture Reading:
Genesis 1, Psalm 30:1-10, Luke 2:44-52

ACTIVATION

Today's prophetic exercise will stretch you. Your assignment is to pray for someone. Now, here are your stipulations. You must pray for at least one person, it must be in public, and it must be audible. YES! You can not be shy today. We are building boldness for purpose, trust me, do NOT skip this exercise. Find one person, they must be in a public place, hold hands with them and pray! Make your prayer a prayer for the revelation of purpose. We are believing God, that as you pray for others' purpose to be revealed, God would reveal yours in an incredible way.

Notes

Day 17

💡 INSPIRATION

Wherever there is purpose, there is a place! Can you say that with me? WHEREVER THERE IS PURPOSE, THERE IS A PLACE (repeat 7 times aloud). We see this in the calling of Abraham. In Genesis, chapter 12, God calls Abraham out of his comfort zone. This is what God is doing with you. You are being called into a certain PLACE. Purpose is only released in the right place. A hammer is only useful in a hand. A song only reaches its potential when it is in the mouth of a great singer. Purpose is only released in the right place. Where there is purpose, there must be placement. Every assignment comes with appointment. During our last lesson we looked at the creational process. One of the things we will notice is that God always creates a place first, and then the person.

And God said, Let there be a firmament in the midst of the waters, and let it divide the waters from the waters. 7 And God made the firmament, and divided the waters which were under the firmament from the waters which were above the firmament: and it was so. 8 And God called the firmament Heaven. And the evening and the morning were the second day. (**Gen. 1:6-8**)

Notice that God creates the sky before He creates the birds. As you continue to read, you will notice that God created the land before He created the beasts of the field. God creates the Garden, before He puts the man in it.

And the LORD God planted a garden eastward in Eden; and there he put the man whom he had formed... And the LORD God took the man, and put him into the garden of Eden to dress it and to keep it. (**Gen. 2:8,15**)

Before Adam moved in his assignment, he needed to be planted in the right place. **The right place unlocks the power of purpose!** Are you in the right place? The significance of placement can never be underestimated. The scripture says that Adam was "put" in the Garden. The word "put" there literally means to appoint. Every assignment comes with appointment. As long as Adam remained in the PLACE, he remained powerful. But as soon as you removed Adam from his place of appointment, everything he does now will be disappointed. Your purpose is demanding you to be planted! BE STABLE!!! What are you doing in your local church? How is your church attendance? How did you pick the church you are attending? These questions are crucial for placement. Wrong placement nullifies purpose.

Is not this the carpenter's son? is not his mother called Mary? and his brethren, James, and Joses, and Simon, and Judas? 56 And his sisters, are they not all with us? Whence then hath this man all these things? 57 And they were offended in him. But Jesus said unto them, A prophet is not without honour, save in his own country, and in his own house. 58 And he did not many mighty works there because of their unbelief. (**Matt. 13:55-58**)

Jesus could not do many mighty works in his hometown. Every anointing has what we call "Active Zones of Ministry." An "active zone" is an atmosphere, place, or geographical location where your ministry thrives. Your purpose is pulling you into a place. Adam's purpose was so tied to the Garden, that after he sinned, and lost revelation of his assignment, he was kicked out of the place. Rejection many times is divine relocation. Rejection is God putting you in the right place so that your purpose will come alive. Your purpose deserves the right place . . . are you willing, like Abraham, to leave your comfort zone to find your "active zone?"

MEDITATION

Concept: GIFTS and CALLINGS (**Matthew 22:14**)

Your purpose never changes. Regardless of place, people, or problem, God has already made up His mind about WHO and WHAT you will be. Your purpose was established before you were even born. If you are in the Earth, you have a purpose. When God gives you an assignment, or purpose, He also gives you GIFTS to help you accomplish your assignment. When we speak about callings, we are speaking of power and place. Has any one of your parents ever called you to do something? The calling was to get your attention and pull you into a particular place. I remember as a young kid, my mom would call my brothers and I to do something. We would reply, "what", but my mom would never answer. When my mother called, she expected us to come to the PLACE of her voice.

For the gifts and calling of God are without repentance. (**Romans 11:29**)

God's gifts and God's call are under full warranty - never canceled, never rescinded. (**Rom. 11:29**, *The Message Version*)

When God calls you, He never changes His mind. Regardless of your mistakes, faults, and failures, God never changes His mind about you! Can you say that with me? GOD HASN'T CHANGED HIS MIND ABOUT ME (repeat aloud 7 times).

Today I want you to ponder on your TALENTS, GIFTS, and CALLING. Take a few moments and meditate on these questions:

1. Am I talented?
2. What are my gifts?
3. What are the top 3 professions that interest me?

4. Am I needed in the church I attend?
5. What is my purpose in the place I am in?
6. Are my gifts being developed?
7. Do I live a life according to the purpose of God in my life?

ACTIVATION

Today's prophetic assignment is simple. Evaluation and scrutinization are valuable ways to assess where you are. Today you will make a list of all your talents, special skills, and gifts. The purpose of this exercise is to get a working list of all the areas of your life and ministry that require focus and attention. Don't let one gift go to waste. I have found out, that when you really step into purpose, all of your talents and gifts will be utilized. You don't have to choose between preaching and poetry, you just have to get in the right place.

Notes

Day 18

💡 INSPIRATION

Mapping out your assignment from God can be difficult, but once done it can produce a level of speed unprecedented. You have never tasted acceleration until you've had a clear understanding of your assignment. Understanding brings acceleration. When we talk about purpose, we are dealing with the confines of your assignment. All of us were born for a reason and for a purpose. There is a specific reason you are here. There is no accident to your arrival. You were born in the right place, at the right time. YOU ARE RIGHT ON SCHEDULE! Can you say this with me? I AM RIGHT ON SCHEDULE (repeat aloud 3 times).

Assignments are not only PLACE SENSITIVE, but assignments are TIME SENSITIVE. Your purpose is not only unleashed in the right place, but your purpose kicks in at the right time. You can ask David! At some point your purpose is going to kick in, and at that point Goliath is coming down. This is why you can never allow your NOW to discourage your FUTURE.

And when the devil had ended all the temptation, he departed from him for a season. (**Luke 4:13**)

We are dealing with time. Notice that Satan came and tempted Jesus for a season. Satan came right before Jesus stepped into purpose. After Jesus was baptized, the scripture says that He was driven, by the Spirit, into the wilderness to be tempted. The right place is called APPOINTMENT, but the right time is called ANOINTING. It is interesting that Jesus never announces His assignment, purpose, or even the fact that He has been anointed until after He has been tried and tested.

The Spirit of the Lord is upon me, because he hath anointed me to preach the gospel to the poor; he hath sent me to heal the brokenhearted, to preach deliverance to the captives, and recovering of sight to the blind, to set at liberty them that are bruised, 19 To preach the acceptable year of the Lord. (**Luke 4:18-19**)

Jesus said that He was anointed to announce The Acceptable Year of the Lord. The Acceptable Year of the Lord was a SET TIME. The Acceptable Year of the Lord referred to the Year of Jubilee, which was a Sabbath of Sabbaths. A jubilee year was the 50th year. In my book, Dirty Knees and Green Thumbs, I elaborate more on the different types of time found in scripture.

Different Types of Time:
1. Right Time
2. Wrong Time
3. Set Time
4. Due Time
5. Out of Due Time
6. Ahead of Time
7. Behind Time
8. Right On Time
9. Seasons
10. Chronos
11. Ages or Dispensations
12. Eternity

Here is an excerpt from my book, Dirty Knees and Green Thumbs, on the subject of a SET TIME,
"Thou shalt arise, and have mercy upon Zion: for the time to favour her, yea, the set time, is come. (Psalm 102:13)

"The concept of a set time is seen throughout the scriptures. This word and/or phrase is mentioned in some way, about 23 times in the King James Version of the Bible. The Hebrew word for "set time" is *mowed* (mow-ed), which means an appointed place or an appointed time. This word also carries with it the connotation of a feast, a sacred moment of time, or a sign. This word can also mean a meeting place."

You are approaching your SET TIME. A set time has already been scheduled in God's calendar. You can't change the date, you can not postpone it, all you can do is arrive. Can I prophesy to you? YOU ARE ABOUT TO ARRIVE!!! There comes a point where all of your hard work, dedication, trials and temptations will push you into your set time. BUT YOU MUST BE PREPARED! Purpose should be prepared for. When you arrive, you don't have time to figure out purpose. When you arrive, the world is expecting you to deliver. There is nothing the enemy can do to stop your set time, but make sure you aren't prepared for it. The articulation of your assignment clarifies your purpose and prepares you for your set time.

MEDITATION

Concept: Predestination (**Eph. 1:11**)

In whom also we have obtained an inheritance, being predestinated according to the purpose of him who worketh all things after the counsel of his own will: (**Eph. 1:11**)

Whenever we begin to discuss predestination, the idea of God preplanning the salvation or damnation of an individual inevitably comes to mind. We must always keep in the forefront of our minds that God is just. Our God is a God of justice, and He is never unjust. IT IS IMPOSSIBLE FOR GOD TO BE UNJUST. God is God alone, and even when we don't understand His ways, He still remains God. We must come to understand that our God is mysterious, and His ways are not always understandable to man. The word predestination literally means that God has "preordained" your destination or destiny. God has established your purpose. It won't change, it won't fade, and it can never be lost. You must have confidence that God knows what He is doing.

Take a moment and ponder on the preordaining power of God. God has established certain things in your life that are out of your control. Take a moment and think about these variables that you had nothing to do with:

1. When were you born?
2. Where were you born?
3. Who are your parents, and what is their history?
4. What family were you born into, and their dynamics.
5. What are my innate strengths and weaknesses?
6. Who are my siblings, and what have they deposited into my development?
7. What are the events surrounding my birth?

Scripture Reading:
Luke 4, Galatians 4:1-6, Psalm 102

ACTIVATION

Today's prophetic assignment is a test of the heart. Today your assignment is to purchase gas for someone. Go to a random gas station and randomly select someone to bless. The amount of gas doesn't matter, it's just the gesture of Christ's love that will bless them.

Day 19

💡 INSPIRATION

When the right place collides with the right time, a moment is created. This moment is the only atmosphere conducive to sustain the birth of destiny. When Jesus came into the Earth, He had to come to the right place at the right time. Jesus was born in a town named Bethlehem. Bethlehem literally means "house of Bread", for this was the place where the Bread of Life was being baked. Jesus grew up in a small town called Nazareth. Nothing spectacular happened here. No one famous came from here. It wasn't "on the map." But while Jesus was in obscurity, there was a young man named John preaching in the hot desert of Judea. John the Baptist was Jesus' elder cousin, by 6 months. I don't like to call John, the Baptist, because he certainly wasn't Baptist according to denominational standards of today. I call him John, the Immerser. John's assignment was to prepare the way for the Messiah. John's job was to create space for the Anointing. John's purpose was to make room for the Christ. John's function was to build Jesus a stage or platform. For every gift, there is ground. For every assignment, there is access. For every purpose, there is a platform. Watch how God does this in the Creative Process:

And God said, Let there be a firmament in the midst of the waters, and let it divide the waters from the waters. (**Gen. 1:6**)

I want you to pay close attention to the word "firmament." This word, "firmament", in the Hebrew literally means space. After God says, "LET THERE BE LIGHT", God then says, "LET THERE BE SPACE!" Wherever there is revelation released, there must be room created. Once you get revelation of your purpose, platforms begin to emerge for you. The only thing standing between you and that OPEN DOOR, is a perfect panoramic perspective of your purpose. You need light in order to shine. SELAH.

And she said unto her husband, Behold now, I perceive that this is an holy man of God, which passeth by us continually. 10 Let us make a little chamber, I pray thee, on the wall; and let us set for him there a bed, and a table, and a stool, and a candlestick: and it shall be, when he cometh to us, that he shall turn in thither. **(2 Kings 4:9-10)**

Did you read that? How dare this woman ask her husband to build a home for another man? Most men would have became irate at the speed of light. But this man understood spiritual things. Couples must be mature spiritually to handle each other's destiny. They proceeded to build a room, a chamber for the Man of God. She created room or space for the prophet. Notice that the scripture says that she built this room "on the wall." Her and her husband literally built this house as an extension of theirs. WATCH ME! The prophet's room was an extension of her house. Now understand, while the prophet is anointed, she runs her house. The platform that she created was an extension of her power. The room was under her rulership. The prophet had space, but the space was laced with levels of authority. Whenever you step on a platform, you must be aware of the fact that you are standing upon someone else's shoulders. Every platform is delegated authority.

Can you think of some platforms, both major and minor, that you have been on in your life? What opportunities, great and small, have defined who you are at this stage of your life? Whose been some gatekeepers and door openers that accelerated your progress? We have all been recipients of God's amazing favor. But I will tell you this, wherever there is favor, there must be honor, or there will be demotion. Honor is the glue that makes favor stick. How is your honor life?

MEDITATION

Concept: The Favor of The Lord (**Luke 1:28**)

LORD, by thy favour thou hast made my mountain to stand strong: thou didst hide thy face, and I was troubled. (**Psalm 30:7**)

I'm God's favorite. He made me king of the mountain." Then you looked the other way and I fell to pieces. (**Psalm 30:7**, *The Message Version*)

The scripture says that Jesus grew in favor with both God and man (Luke 2:52). The favor that comes from man is good. God will use men to open doors to creates moments of exposure. Man does have promotion power, but only within the systems of men. True promotion comes from the Lord (Psalm 75:6). The favor that comes from God is unprecedented. The favor that comes from God is not momentary. One moment of God's favor will change your entire life. Can you believe God for raw favor. Favor is when God shows you, "HEY! I'M FOR YOU!" God wants you to know that He is for you. It is important to note the second part of this verse. It says, "then you looked the other way and I fell to pieces." This denotes that favor is when God looks in your direction. WOW! Did you feel that? Favor is when God looks in your direction! Can we prophesy? GOD IS ABOUT TO LOOK IN YOUR DIRECTION!!! Take a few moments to ponder on the favor of the Lord. Regardless of where it came from, man or a Sovereign move, God is at the center of real favor. Can you recall any moments of divine favor in your life? Can you remember any time a door was opened for you that changed your life? Take a few moments to think on these things.

Scripture Reading:
Luke 1:23-33, Psalm 30, 2 Kings 4:4-14

ACTIVATION

Today your prophetic assignment is simple, it is to give someone a chance. At some point God gave you a chance. Can you take a moment and thank God for another chance? Do this aloud. Yes, I will wait . . . Did you do it? Today show someone favor. This can take place in a few ways, here are a few examples:

1. Let someone get in front of you in a line.
2. Send someone a special appreciation gift.
3. Sow a seed into someone's life.
4. Take someone out to dinner.
5. Babysit someone's children for free.
6. If you own a business, give away something for free.
7. Leave money in a place where someone can find it.

Notes

Day 20

💡 INSPIRATION

Congratulations! You have officially reached the halfway point. Completing assignments, being consistent, meeting deadlines, and investing in oneself are truly the marks of a world changer. As we conclude this session on the subject of purpose, let us be mindful that purpose must be revealed, accepted, developed, empowered, and dissected. You have a responsibility to be possessed with purpose. Purpose can not be a frivolous subject in the life of the Believer. Purpose must be a top priority.

Purpose demands discovery. Purpose requires exploration. Whenever God reveals something about Himself, or something about you, He is inviting you into a world of exploration. We see this all throughout the Old Testament. God would strategically, at divine moments, reveal a facet of Himself to Israel. Whenever God shows you a particular dimension of His character, understand that He is unlocking a world to you. All of us are "multi-sided" beings. We are all multi-dimensional creatures. We have feelings, thoughts, opinions, dispositions, attitudes, and on top of all of that, we have a purpose. For instance you may be a sister, wife, and a mother. While you are a mother to your children, you are not a mother to everyone. Everyone doesn't get the honor of seeing that side or dimension of you. If you show someone that side, you are inviting them into that world. When someone sees this side of you, for instance, you changing a diaper, this is called revelation. Revelation unlocks our perception, and gives us the power of knowledge. WATCH ME! Because once I know something, I can't "unknow" it. See this is why the devil is afraid of you ever coming into the revelation of your purpose. Once you see it, you must become it.

And Moses built an altar, and called the name of it Jehovahnissi: 16 For he said, Because the LORD hath sworn that the LORD will have war with Amalek from generation to generation. (**Exodus 17:15-16**)

In Exodus, chapter 17, Israel is met with their first battle as a nation. Israel has been delivered by God's supernatural power, they have received the Ten Commandments, written by the finger of God, but now they have to get dirty. Purpose requires you to shed the facade of fantasy and live in reality. The reality of life is that greatness never just happens. If you want GREATNESS, you must be willing to pierce the membrane called MEDIOCRITY. YOU MUST BREAK MEDIOCRITY! Can you say this with me? I WILL NOT BE MEDIOCRE (repeat 7 times aloud). Around your purpose there is a small layer of resistance called opposition. Opposition is purposeful. The butterfly gains strength as it fights its way out of the cocoon. A chick gains power as it pecks its way out of the egg. As you press into purpose, through haters, phony friends, and outright enemies, you are gaining the strength you need for this amazing journey called purpose.

Israel had to learn a valuable lesson: Good things come to those who wait, but great things are reserved for those who fight! In Exodus, chapter 17, God reveals Himself as Jehovah Nissi. This covenant name of God literally means, "The Lord is my Standard or Banner." In the days of Old, every army carried an ensign to promote the nation or king they were defending. This banner, if the army was well equipped, could incite fear at its very sight. Jesus is our banner. Jesus is our ensign. Whenever we go into battle, we carry our flag, which is Jesus, this is why He was crucified on a pole. SELAH! And trust me, when all of Hell sees our banner, they cower in absolute panic. The name Jehovah Nissi, doesn't mean that Jesus is just our flag, but it literally says that Jesus is our victory. DID YOU HEAR THAT? You don't have to try to win, Jesus won for you. We are not trying to win the battle, Jesus has already won the battle. SO WHY AM I STRUGGLING PASTOR? Because you are still fighting. Selah.

Purpose blossoms as we recognize the spiritual victories in our life. As we look back over our battles, it becomes very easy to see that God has always had a purpose for our life. Our God is a God of purpose. God wants your life to be mark by victories, not failures. Today begins a string of victories in your life that will propel you into the depths of your purpose.

MEDITATION

Concept: The Covenant Names of the Lord (**Proverbs 18:10**)

Throughout the scripture, God would choose strategic times to reveal certain truths about Himself and facets of His character. God always reveals His character through the unveiling of a covenant name. Once God revealed His name, He was making a covenant with His people that He would be "that", whatever the name depicted, in their life. So if God revealed Himself as Jehovah Nissi, then Israel understand that no enemy could defeat them. If God revealed Himself as Jehovah Jireh, then Israel understood that God would be their money. When God reveals to you a name, He expects for you to run into that dimension to find safety and confidence. Here are some Covenant names of the Lord:
1. Jehovah-Jireh "The Lord will Provide" (Genesis 22:14).
2. Jehovah-Nissi "The Lord is my Banner" (Exodus 17:15).

3. Jehovah-Mekaddesh "The Lord Sanctifies" (Exodus 31:13).
4. Jehovah-Shalom "The Lord is Peace" (Judges 6:24).
5. Jehovah-Sabaoth "The Lord of Hosts" (1 Samuel 1:3; Jeremiah 11:20).
6. Jehovah-Rohi "The Lord is my Shepherd" (Psalm 23:1).
7. Jehovah-Tsidkenu "The Lord is Our Righteousness" (Jeremiah 23:5-6; Jeremiah 33:16).
8. Jehovah-Shammah "The Lord is There" (Ezekiel 48:35)

Take a moment and ponder on the Covenant Names of the Lord. What names have you personally encountered? What names are you yet to encounter? Just because one may be familiar with a name, doesn't mean one has encountered it. Everyone of the covenant names of the Lord must become your reality. Take a moment and meditate on the moments God revealed Himself to you in an incredible way.

Scripture Reading:
Exodus 17, Psalm 18:5-15, John 8:53-59

ACTIVATION

Today's prophetic assignment is designed to build your muscle of memorization. Your assignment today is to choose three scriptures. Each scripture should not be longer than three verses, and these scriptures you will commit to memory. These three verses will be your life's verses. Your ministry, family, and business will surround these verses. Put these verses on your refrigerator, in your office, on your bathroom mirror, any and everywhere you can, to always remind yourself of God's Word over your life.

Session Five: Power

Day 21

💡 INSPIRATION

Today we begin a new string of studies on the subject of power. Once purpose is understood, power is needed. Power is transformative energy. Power is defined as the ability to bring change. Change is true transformation. Power is defined as work divided by time. Power is determined by how much work can be done over a particular span of time. During this session we begin to turn our attention towards your ability.

Now unto him that is able to do exceeding abundantly above all that we ask or think, according to the power that worketh in us (**Eph. 3:20**)

Pay close attention to the world "able." This verse of scripture is speaking of God's ability and/or power. What one is "able" to do is their ability. This verse also says that there is power in us. What is this power? All human beings are born equipped with three types of power: the ability to think, the power to speak, and gift power. The way we think has the ability to change the world. How we speak has the ability to impart life or death (**Prov. 18:21**). God also gives each human being the power of creativity. Through our thinking, our speaking, and through our creativity, we have the ability to bring change to the world in which we live. Power is given.

God hath spoken once; twice have I heard this; that power belongeth unto God. (**Psalm 62:11**)

Can you say this with me, ALL POWER BELONGS TO GOD (repeat aloud 7 times). It is important that we wrap our theology around the fact that all power belongs to God. God gives power.

And when he had called unto him his twelve disciples, he gave them power... (**Matthew 10:1**)

Power is given. God gives power. Power is only given for purpose. Power without purpose turns into anarchy. This is why power must only come with maturity. Power can not be given to juveniles. How do you manage power? How do you manage your thoughts, your words, and your gifts? God expects us to be good stewards over anything committed into our care. Power must be respected. The moment power isn't respected, it turns on you. God gives power for purpose. God is bringing you into a season of power, with respect. When a person doesn't respect power, they will think anything, speak whatever they please, and create out of lust. Your respect for power is seen in how you steward your thoughts, your words, and your work. Remember, power is work over time. How do you view time? Are you constantly late? If so, this means you do not respect time. Power must be respected. Our respect for power can be measured in how we manage our work, and our time. Do we strive for excellence? Are we comfortable being mediocre? Before we access the dimensions of power, we have to respect the power God has already given. GOT POWER?

MEDITATION

Concept: The Law of the Conservation of Energy

The Law of the Conservation of Energy is a law of science that states that energy cannot be created or destroyed, but only changed from one form into another or transferred from one object to another. If we had time, I would show you how this law manages the movement of mantles (we will save that for another time). This law deals with the way power travels. Within a closed system, which is any system with laws, energy or power never leaves, it only shifts hands. As far back as Empedocles, great thinkers have understood this. In 1638, Galileo built upon this concept as well. But it was Gottfried Wilhelm von Leibniz, between the years of 1676–1689, that finally formulated a formula to articulate and capture this principle. This law is very important in understanding that power is never lost, it just moves.

Today, take a moment to meditate on how power has moved in your life. What are some of your strengths? What are some of your weaknesses? What are areas of your life that you lean on the most, especially in difficult times? Take a moment and ponder these questions:

1. What is my attention capacity?
2. How is my creativity being cultivated?
3. What is the maturity of my mouth?
4. Are my thoughts subject to Christ?
5. What are my strengths?
6. Where is my "Achilles Heel" or weakness located?
7. When was the last time I upgraded my vocabulary?

Scripture Reading:
Matthew 10:1-6, Ephesians 3:15-21, Psalm 62

ACTIVATION

Today's prophetic exercise is an activity that will challenge your creativity. Find a creative way to explain, demonstrate, and share the Law of the Conservation of Energy.

Day 22

💡 INSPIRATION

Power is not just given. Power is entered. Power must be accessed. You must be processed into power. Power is not for the insecure, nor is it for the arrogant. **Receiving power without a process only further amplifies a person's dysfunction.** Power must be respected. The respect of power is called honor. Being able to celebrate and respect another person's rank, authority, and level of gifting, is the key to properly managing power. Ask Saul! Jealousy and comparison will always nullify the power that is present. Power requires honor. Honor keeps the heart humble during Power's performance. It's very easy to allow power to go to your head. This is what happened to Satan.

How art thou fallen from heaven, O Lucifer, son of the morning! how art thou cut down to the ground, which didst weaken the nations! 13 For thou hast said in thine heart, I will ascend into heaven, I will exalt my throne above the stars of God: I will sit also upon the mount of the congregation, in the sides of the north: 14 I will ascend above the heights of the clouds; I will be like the most High. **(Isa. 14:12-14)**

Satan started off as one of the chief cherubim. His job was to guard the glory of God, reflect revelation, inspire and orchestrate worship within the Heavenly temple, and to maintain the Holy Place. But something happens when power goes to our head. In Isaiah, chapter 14, it shows that Satan declares emphatically, "I will!" This is a dangerous statement within the confines of ministry blocks. Ministry is not about you! When God gives power, it is to empower others. Power is never for ourselves. Can you say that with me? MY

POWER IS NOT FOR ME (please repeat 5 times aloud). If you are in ministry, aspire to serve the Lord in any capacity, and/or are a leader in your local assembly, you must repeatedly do an attitude check. Your heart is where your power flows from, if your heart isn't right, your anointing will be infected. Notice that verse thirteen says that Satan declared this within his own heart. Listen to me carefully, DO NOT LIE TO YOURSELF. What are you saying to yourself in your own heart? Humility is having a correct and sober perspective about ourselves. Humility is not seeing yourself lower than you are, but seeing yourself actually where you are. Humility is all about honesty. Arrogant people are just great liars who've found a way to convince themselves that they're better than they truly are.

For I say, through the grace given unto me, to every man that is among you, not to think of himself more highly than he ought to think; but to think soberly, according as God hath dealt to every man the measure of faith. (**Romans 12:3**)

The apostle Paul was a phenomenal mind. Notice here that Paul begins his statement by saying, "for I say, through the grace given unto me." Did you see that? Paul is saying that the only reason he can make such a statement, is because at some point he received grace. The apostle Paul didn't start off a nice guy. You may have not either, but isn't it great that God gives grace to mean people. But Paul states that it is grace that gave him the ability to say this. Paul says, "through grace" am I saying this. I believe Paul was very much acquainted with arrogance and pride, and understood their destructive powers. God will humble you if he needs to.

Even though we can list what many might think are impressive credentials. You know my pedigree: 5 a legitimate birth, circumcised on the eighth day; an Israelite from the elite tribe of Benjamin; a strict and devout adherent to God's law; 6 a fiery defender of the purity of my religion, even to the point of persecuting Christians; a meticulous observer of everything set down in God's law Book. 7 The very credentials these people are waving around as something special, I'm tearing up and throwing out with the trash - along with everything else I used to take credit for. And why? Because of Christ. (**Phil. 3:4-7**, The Message)

Paul's past was filled with pride and arrogance, but God will humble you. Humility is the key to the effective use of power. Power must be coupled with humility, otherwise the user is slowly polluted, never realizing that the intents and motives of their heart has slowly changed. No one prays for humility. No one ever says, "Pastor, can you do a series on humility." Pride is preached. Now I believe in the confidence of the Kingdom. I believe everyone who has named Jesus as their Lord should be confident, but not in themselves, in the Lord. I am confident in Jesus the Christ. Humility is maintained by keeping Christ in view. God wants to give you power, but He doesn't want that power to go to your head. God would rather you be a humble "nobody" than a prideful "somebody."

Pride goeth before destruction, and an haughty spirit before a fall. (**Prov. 16:18**)

MEDITATION

Concept: The 5 "I WILLS" of Satan (**Isa. 14:12-15**)

Thou wast perfect in thy ways from the day that thou wast created, till iniquity was found in thee. (**Ezekiel 28:15**)

It was hard, as a new Believer, for me to wrap my theology around the "Satan situation." I never doubted his existence, like many Christians do today, for I understand the principle of polarity. It's the Law of Opposites. We see this system within nature. There is hot, and cold. There is day, and night. There is male, and female. There is up, and there is down. And if you are disoriented, gravity will remind you which way is down. If there is good, there must be evil. I understood Satan's existence. What was hard for me to understand was his sin. Satan was in Heaven, where did sin come from? Isaiah, chapter 14, says that Satan said "I will" in his own heart. Ezekiel, chapter 28, says "iniquity was found in thee." The word "iniquity" is the word `evel in Hebrew. Notice how it looks very similar to the English word "evil." This word literally means injustice of speech. WOW. Did you read that? What Satan said in his heart was unjust, and that produced the iniquity. Satan's comment was unjust because God had provided everything for him, and he was still ungrateful. Iniquity literally means a bending or crooked place. Iniquity is perversion. Iniquity is our patterns of perversion locked within our DNA. They are usually passed down through families and cultures. Satan made five "I WILL" statements:

1. **"I will** ascend into Heaven." - Now Satan is already in Heaven, but he is referencing the very dwelling place of God, or God's throne. He want to take God's place.
2. **"I will** exalt my throne above the stars of God." - What Satan was saying here is, "I will rule angels."
3. **"I will** sit also upon the mount of the congregation in the sides of the north." - This is Earth as a place. Satan was saying here that he would rule mankind.
4. **"I will** ascend above the heights of the clouds." - He wills to displace God as the Sovereign of the universe. Clouds in the scripture usually speaks to the Saints of Old. Satan could have been saying that he wanted to be over the church.
5. **"I will** be like the Most High." - Now Satan has gone too far. He now compares himself with the Almighty. This is pride on its highest level. Comparison is a interesting phenomenon. Comparison is pride and insecurity. SELAH!

Take a moment and ponder on pride. Is there any pride in your life? How has God humbled you? Can you recall an event that revealed pride in your life? Has anyone ever said that you struggle with pride? What are some ways in which you can remain humble? What is your concept of humility?

ACTIVATION

Today your prophetic exercise is a test of your humility. Today is a day of service. Here is your prophetic assignment. Find a stranger, co-worker, friend, or colleague and ask them if you can do something significant for them. This doesn't have to include money, but it can. Here are some great ideas that you can use:

1. Send someone a random card of appreciation.
2. Make someone a creative gift that honors their contribution.
3. Open the door for everyone today.
4. Start every conversation with, "what I like about you."
5. Randomly give out hugs in your workplace.
6. Share today's MENTORSHIP PACKAGE with 10 people

Notes

Day 23

💡 INSPIRATION

For the kingdom of heaven is as a man travelling into a far country, who called his own servants, and delivered unto them his goods. (**Matt. 25:14**)

This is one of my favorite verses of scripture. In this parable of the Kingdom, Jesus shows us how the Kingdom of Heaven is structured. "For the kingdom of heaven is as a man …", this is a powerful statement. When we begin to look at the makeup of man, and how man was built, there are a few things we must consider.

What? know ye not that your body is the temple of the Holy Ghost which is in you, which ye have of God, and ye are not your own? (**1 Cor. 6:19**)

Your body is a temple. When God built Adam, He was building a dwelling place or temple. After God delivered the children of Israel from Egypt, He took them into the Wilderness, and there commanded Moses to construct a temple. This temple was called the tabernacle, and was a place for God to meet with man. The Hebrew term for this place is called *OHEL MOED*. This term denotes a meeting place, a gathering place, or a rendezvous location. It literally means an appointed place or sacred time. The tabernacle, or temple, was a place where God met with man. When God commands Moses to build the tabernacle, this is what he says,

According to all that I shew thee, after the pattern of the tabernacle, and the pattern of all the instruments thereof, even so shall ye make it. (**Ex. 25:6**)

God didn't want Moses to build the tabernacle according to his own imagination. Remember, God is a God of specifics. The Lord commanded that Moses build the Tabernacle in the Earth, according to the blueprint in Heaven. What schematic do you think God used to build Adam? It was the same blueprint. God used the Heavenly temple to construct man's body. "For the kingdom of heaven is as a man …", this statement should take on a new meaning now. When Moses built the Tabernacle, he started with the head, or the Ark of the Covenant. Everything God does, He does head first. When a baby is born, it is born head first. When God created Adam, I believe He started with his head. Why is this important? Because Adam was a thinking being. The kingdom of God is like a man in the sense that it is a thinking kingdom. The kingdom of God is not a system of ignorance. The kingdom of God functions by divine education. The kingdom of God is a thinking system. Can you say this with me? I AM A THINKER (please repeat 7 time aloud).

Thinking is a power source. In the scripture, there are many forms of power. Some of these different forms of power are seen here,

And what is the exceeding greatness of his power to us-ward who believe, according to the working of his mighty power, 20 Which he wrought in Christ, when he raised him from the dead, and set him at his own right hand in the heavenly places (**Eph.1:19-20**)

Now when you look at this verse in Greek, we notice that there are four different Greek words for "power" used here. Here is another look at the verse,

*And what is the exceeding greatness of his power (**dunamis**) to us-ward who believe, according to the working (**energeia**) of his mighty (**ischus**) power (**kratos**), Which he wrought (**energeia**) in Christ, when he raised him from*

the dead, and set him at his own right hand in the heavenly places (**Eph. 1:19-20**)

Notice that there are four different Greek words used for "power." These are four different dimensions of power, but there are a total of five dimensions of power:

1. ***Exousia*-** This is delegated authority. This Greek word can be seen in Matthew, chapter 8 and verse 9, and it means authority or authorized power. This is power that is given. This word means the power of choice, judicial authority, and/or the realm of jurisdiction. Exousia is the power of representation. A familiar example of this is a law enforcement officer. Every police officer has both a gun, and a badge. The gun gives them power, but the badge gives them authority. Exousia is the power of the badge.
2. ***Dunamis*-** This is the power zone most of us are familiar with. Dunamis is miracle power. Jesus told the disciples, in Acts chapter 1, to go and wait in Jerusalem until they be given power. Jesus was referring to dunamis. This is explosive power. We get the word dynamite from this Greek word. Dunamis refers to raw miracle power. Dunamis is the explosive energy felt from Heaven entering Earth. This is also known as spirit power.
3. ***Energeia*-** This Greek word denotes efficiency. This word literally means to work. As you can see, this is where we get the word energy from. This is system power. Energeia is systemic power. Energeia is the power that is seen within a closed organization. It's the way a system works, and the power it produces. For instance, most fast food restaurants have a system. Once you place your order, the system goes to work. The strength of the system determines how fast I get

my food, if my food is hot, and if my order is correct. If there is a problem in the system, the product will be wrong. Energeia is systemic power.

4. ***Ischus-*** This is might! The Greek word means ability, force, strength, or might. God spoke to Gideon, in Judges chapter 6, and said, "Go in this thy might." We all have a might. It is innate power and ability. Your might is made up of your physical strength, your intellectual capacity, and your will. There are some assignments that God gives to us, and like Gideon, we have to solve them with our might.

5. ***Kratos-*** This is dominion power. This Greek word literally means a mighty deed, a work of power or demonstration, and/or raw dominion. When God created man, He blessed man and told man to "have dominion." This was a dimension of power. This is ruling power or the ability to bring something under subjection. Kratos is impact power. Kratos deals with the impact, and the imprint left as an effect. This is where we get the word crater from.

MEDITATION

Nearly all men can stand adversity, but if you want to test a man's character, give him power.
-Abraham Lincoln

All the forces in the world are not so powerful as an idea whose time has come.
-Victor Hugo

Today ponder on the power of God. Power is an interesting concept. What are some moments in your life where you saw power used, and/or abused? What was your first encounter with the power of

God? When was the last time you saw an authentic miracle? Power is all around us, but power must be recognized, respected, and then received. Take a few moments and ponder on the power of God, and its significance in your life.

Scripture Reading:
Ephesians 1, Matthew 8:4-14, Matthew 28:13-20

ACTIVATION

Today's activation is a test of your obedience. Mentorship is all about following directions, evaluations, and ultimately, making adjustments. While the student performs, the mentor judges and then makes adjustments where and when they are needed. Your prophetic assignment today is to perform a miracle. WHAT? Yes, your assignment today is to approach a stranger, ask them what they are in need of, and then stand with them in prayer and in faith. Join them in their journey into the miraculous. God is calling you to a new level of power. Trust Him in this assignment, be bold, miracles are coming.

Notes

Day 24

💡 INSPIRATION

Power has a language. Power and the mouth are irrevocably tied together. We see this in the Beginning during the creative process. The first time we get a glimpse of God's power, He is speaking. There is darkness. Silence. No one around. And all of a sudden, out of the abyss of nothingness, comes a sound . . . "Let light be!" Now we don't know if God whispered, or if His voice thundered throughout the cosmos. But when God said, "Let there be light" understand that there was a divine reaction. Whenever power speaks, there must be a response. God is so awesome that when He spoke, things that hadn't even come into being yet responded. There is an ancient Hebrew concept surrounding this event. In Hebrew, light is associated with order. This is why the preceding verses speak of disorder. When God said, "Let light be", this was an order issue. Genesis, chapter 1 and verse 3, could be translated, "let there be order." Power is only safe within order. Power without order becomes anarchy and creates dictatorships. Order is the proper arrangement of things. Order is correct placement. Power only empowers when there is order. When there is no order, power destroys. Have you ever been a victim of the power of disorder? The Spirit of Chaos in your life must be broken. Your life demands order. Take a moment now, and pray this prayer aloud with me:

Father, I repent for allowing disorder in my life. Father, I repent for all acts of sin, rebellion, willful disobedience, blatant dishonor, and a lack of kingdom order. Father, in the name of Jesus, release my life from destructive cycles, and release order like you did in Genesis, chapter one. Father, speak order into my life! Father, in the name of Jesus, I ask that you break all patterns of disorder in my life. All spirits of chaos, confusion, and demonic curiosity, be broken now in Jesus' name. Any system contrary to your purpose and plan for my life, render it powerless now. I ask that you renew my mind according to your word, so that my thought life would be in order. Renew my eyes, so that my vision would be in order. Renew my mouth, so that my words would be in order. It is in Jesus name I pray, Amen.

Power speaks. Wherever there is power, there will always be a command.

For I am a man under authority, having soldiers under me: and I say to this man, Go, and he goeth; and to another, Come, and he cometh; and to my servant, Do this, and he doeth it. 10 When Jesus heard it, he marvelled, and said to them that followed , Verily I say unto you, I have not found so great faith, no, not in Israel. (**Matt. 8:9-10**)

Power and the mouth are irrevocably tied together. Authentic authority never works by force, it works by command. Adam walked in this power. Adam had declarative power. Whatever Adam spoke became law. This is the power that Adam walked in.

Thou madest him to have dominion over the works of thy hands; thou hast put all things under his feet: (**Psalm 8:6**)

And out of the ground the LORD God formed every beast of the field, and every fowl of the air; and brought them unto Adam to see what he would call them: and whatsoever Adam called every living creature, that was the name thereof. (**Gen. 2:19**)

Adam was able to name the birds of the sky, the animals of the field, and even the creatures on the ocean floor, Adam named them too. Power speaks. Wherever you see power, you will hear a sound. This is powerfully demonstrated in Acts, chapter 2. After Jesus, who is The

Word (notice the connection to the mouth), has been crucified, buried, and resurrected. He has shown himself alive for 40 days, by many infallible proofs (Acts 1:3), and has now commanded that His disciples wait in Jerusalem to receive power.

NOTE: Here is a lesson in mentorship. Obedience is the key in the development of a leader. Leadership is about leading, and to lead you must become a great follower. Real recognizes real. Power recognizes power. Greatness recognizes greatness. Greatness is locked in your ability to obey. Leaders who have never followed can never truly produce followers. What is your level of submission? Where does your loyalty reside? Is your authority valid? Who gave it to you? Your strength as a leader is locked in your submission to authority. Find somewhere to serve.

After the disciples waited for 10 days, all of a sudden they heard a sound. Power speaks. In Acts, chapter 2, all of the disciples were filled with the Holy Spirit and began to speak with tongues. This was a sign that they had received power. Power has a language. The language of the Kingdom is the language of the Holy Spirit.

And when the day of Pentecost was fully come, they were all with one accord in one place. **2** And suddenly there came a sound from heaven as of a rushing mighty wind, and it filled all the house where they were sitting. **3** And there appeared unto them cloven tongues like as of fire, and it sat upon each of them. **4** And they were all filled with the Holy Ghost, and began to speak with other tongues, as the Spirit gave them utterance (Acts 2:1-4).

MEDITATION

Concept: Praying in the Spirit (**1 Cor. 14:2**)

There is much debate around the subject of Glossolalia, or speaking in other tongues. I believe the scripture is very clear on this subject, and that every Believer should search the scripture and seek to experience the Baptism of the Holy Spirit. Not only is tongues the effect and byproduct of the resident dwelling of the Holy Spirit within a person. But speaking in tongues is a form of power. The scripture is clear that praying in the spirit builds up the Believer.

But ye, beloved, building up yourselves on your most holy faith, praying in the Holy Ghost (**Jude 1:20**)

The Baptism of the Holy Spirit is a subsequent experience to Salvation. After you are born again, it is imperative that you seek the Baptism of the Holy Spirit. The first Baptism of the Believer is in water, for the remission of sins. The second Baptism is in the Holy Ghost, for the deposit of power. Praying in the Holy Spirit allows us to bypass our intellect, our enemies, and our understanding, and speak directly in the ear of God. Praying in tongues is a weapon for every Believer.

Today I want you to ponder on the power of God in speech. Can you think of any instances in your life where power was demonstrated by speech? Who has vocal authority in your life? Whose voice paralyzes you? Take a moment and ponder on these questions:

1. Have I received the Baptism of the Holy Spirit?
2. Does the church I attend believe in speaking and or praying in tongues?

3. Do I understand the purpose of praying in the Spirit?
4. How often do I pray in tongues?
5. What benefits does praying in the spirit bring?
6. Have I studied this subject enough to have faith in this area?
7. How can I utilize praying in the spirit to a greater degree in my life?

Scripture Reading:
Acts 2:1-8, 1 Corinthians 14:9-19, Psalm 8

ACTIVATION

Today's prophetic assignment is designed to stretch your endurance and unlock mysteries. Your exercise today is to pray in the spirit for **TEN MINUTES**. Remember, this is an exercise and may take some practice. You can do this on your lunch break, in traffic, or find a nice quiet place now. Power speaks. This should NOT be done silently, but should be audible. Time yourself, log your experience, expect miracles.

Notes

_____
_____
_____
_____
_____
_____
_____
_____
_____
_____

Day 25

💡 INSPIRATION

Today we conclude session five. In session five we addressed our understanding of power. Power is responsibility. Power is weight. Power requires stewardship. Power demands respect. Power is not only given, power is entered. Power is a subject that would take us years to exhaust. As we conclude session five, we focus in on management. Power must be managed. Let's look at the Adamic Model:

And the LORD God took the man, and put him into the garden of Eden to dress it and to keep it. (**Gen. 2:15**)

This verse is loaded with significance. With every assignment, a certain measure of power must be given. This measure of power is called one's measure or jurisdiction. The Garden was Adam's jurisdiction. It was in the Garden where Adam had power. It was in the Garden, where Adam had authority. Now inside the Garden, Adam is the man. Outside the Garden, Adam is ordinary. Within the Garden, Adam's gifts are working at 100 percent. Outside the Garden, Adam's gifts begin to depreciate, and his flaws are exposed. It is important that we all find the Garden for our gift. Everyone has a measure. We all have a rule of power. One's rule of power is usually established by the Giver of power, and can be increased by stewardship. When Adam was placed in the Garden, he was given two jobs: to tend it, and keep it. The word "tend" here in the Hebrew literally means to cultivate, grow, and/or expand. Your measure can increase. Can you say that with me? MY MEASURE IS INCREASING NOW (repeat 3 times aloud). Regardless of where you are, you can increase. Not only do all of us have a responsibility to tend and grow our place of influence, but God also told Adam to "keep" the Garden. The word "keep" means to defend and protect. Your Garden is your safe place, it's your place of development, the womb of your ministry, it must be protected.

Power never comes without responsibility. With every Garden comes responsibility. When God created Adam, God gave Adam a huge responsibility.

What is man, that thou art mindful of him? and the son of man, that thou visitest him? 5 For thou hast made him a little lower than the angels, and hast crowned him with glory and honour. 6 Thou madest him to have dominion over the works of thy hands; thou hast put all things under his feet: (**Psalm 8:4-6**)

When God established Adam, He gave Adam dominion. God gave Adam the responsibility of stewarding "all the works of His hands." Adam was at the top of the food chain. Adam was the boss. The scripture says that God gave Adam two things, glory and honor. Glory literally means the weight of responsibility. In the days of Old, the priest would carry the Ark of God, which was made of wood and overlaid with Gold, throughout their wanderings. This box of Glory was heavy, and took a team to carry. Why? Because glory is a weighty thing. Responsibility is measured in what we call pressure. It is this pressure that crushes the minister and extracts the oil for ministry. You don't get oil without responsibility. Whenever God gives glory, He must simultaneously give rank. Honor is rank. The scripture says that God crowned Adam with honor. Honor is the Hebrew word "*hadar,*" and it literally means rank. Rank is raw authority. Rank is the measure of one's influence. The greater the responsibility, the greater the rank. If you want to increase in rank, ask God for more responsibility!

God wants to address your rank. Every gift has a rank. Every anointing has a rank. Every presentation and performance has rank. The kingdom of God is a system of order. Wherever there is order, there will be rank and file. This is an important concept within the kingdom. While we are all equally loved by God, we are not all equally anointed by God. The anointing is given according to assignment. Power is given according to responsibility. How do you know where your measure stops? How do you know where you rank ends? How do you know the boundaries of your Garden? Where your competence ends! See every platform has lights. The greater the platform, the brighter the lights. The brighter the lights, the more imperfections that are seen. Once your gifts begins to breakdown under the pressure of a platform, that is a sign that you have reached the edge of your Garden. Once you reach the edge of you Garden, you then have the responsibility of INCREASING YOUR MEASURE. This is called the process of dominion.

MEDITATION

Responsibility is the price of freedom.
-Elbert Hubbard

Freedom makes a huge requirement of every human being. With freedom comes responsibility. For the person who is unwilling to grow up, the person who does not want to carry his own weight, this is a frightening prospect.
-Eleanor Roosevelt

Today I want you to ponder on the beauty of responsibility. Some people love responsibility, and others run away from responsibility. With freedom comes responsibility. The only life that requires no responsibility is the life of a slave. When the children of Israel were in Egypt, they never had to worry about what they were going to eat or wear. This is the blessing of slavery. Within the confines of slavery, all your needs are met. Within the confines of slavery, your purpose is pushed on you. But in freedom, you have the responsibility to feed and clothe yourself. In freedom, you have to discover your purpose and work your potential. In honesty, most people enjoy slavery more than freedom, because slavery doesn't come with responsibility.

Today ponder the blessing and beauty of responsibility. What are some areas God has made you responsible for? How are you managing those areas? How are you increasing your measure of rule? Are you actively involved with widening your area of influence? Take a moment and meditate on your Garden.

Scripture Reading:
Genesis 2, 2 Corinthians 10:9-18, Jude 1:4-14

ACTIVATION

Today, your prophetic assignment is to map out the borders of your Garden. Find a quiet place, this may take some research and time, but make a list of all the things you do well, and all the things you don't do well. Please, be honest. Please focus your list on ministry, family, your gift, and anointing. Here are some questions that will help guide this process:

1. When am I most confident?
2. When am I most nervous?
3. How does my nervousness manifest?
4. When do my weaknesses show the most?
5. What platform highlights my strengths?
6. When was the last time my life increased in responsibility?
7. What happens to me, and my life, when I am stressed?

After you have formulated a workable list of things you do well, and things you don't do so well, identify where and when these gifts or skills function at their optimum level. This place is called your Garden. As you track where your gift begins to lose strength and focus, this reveals the end of your jurisdiction. This is your assignment.

Notes

Session Six: Personality

THE JOURNEY

Day 26

💡 INSPIRATION

Whenever God anoints an individual, that anointing mixes with their personality, creating a chemical compound that is only unique to them. While the Kingdom of God is a system of order, we pride ourselves on highlighting the vastness and diversity of God. God is in the business of raising up originals, and not copies. As we enter session six, we begin to focus on the personality. In this session we will delve into the crevices of your creativity, and navigate through the nooks of your nature. We are all wired a particular way. I am not talking about our understanding of the world, or gender roles, those things are learned. But we are all born with a particular leaning. Our gifts lean a particular way, our appetites lean a certain way, and even our attention leans a certain way by nature of our personality. I believe that the personality is something that we should address, discover, and develop. There is a reason God called YOU! There is a reason why God has given you a specific assignment in the Body of Christ, that no one can accomplish but you. You are unique. You are needed. Can you say that with me? I AM NEEDED IN THE KINGDOM (please repeat 5 times aloud).

Let no man despise thy youth; but be thou an example of the believers, in word, in conversation, in charity, in spirit, in faith, in purity. (1 Timothy 4:12)

Paul had such an affinity for Timothy. Timothy was Paul's son in the ministry. Paul had groomed Timothy and spent significant time shaping his future. Timothy was a very young man, and this caused some trepidation in his heart. "Can God use me?" I'm sure this question filled his mind. Just like this question has filled yours. One thing that I love about God, is that when God calls you, HE CALLS YOU! God wants you for you. He knew all of your issues, secrets, weaknesses, and frailties, and guess what? He still called you. Confidence is never produced by competition, only comparison is. Only when you truly accept what makes you different, does your anointing shift from generic to authentic. In this season, God wants you to focus on what makes you unique. The celebration of our uniqueness is called honor.

The Kingdom of God is a system of empowerment. God empowers man with Gifts, Anointings, Callings, and Talents to advance the rule of Jesus Christ in the Earth. Now it is important that we understand the function of all four of these.

GIFTS- A gift is a key that opens doors to bring you into the presence of great men. Your gift is Sovereignly given by God. Most times you gift can not be traced through blood. It is a divine deposit.

ANOINTINGS- An anointing is a special endowment of enabling power that gives you the ability to complete your assignment once you are in front of these great men.

CALLINGS- Calling imparts identity and confidence to operate in the anointing that God places upon your life. It's your destiny, mixed with your uniqueness to create an authentic assignment.

TALENTS- Talents are lower level or lower dimensional gifts that undergird your dominant gift to bring support and balance. Your talents are usually transferred through DNA.

The development of your personality is just as important as the development of your Biblical knowledge and your anointing. Throughout the years, I have seen the damage that a weak personality can cause. I have seen an under developed personality split churches, break up families, and even ruin ministries with no hope of restoration. Your personality deserves your attention. In this session, get ready for a prophetic journey into the tunnels of your temperament.

MEDITATION

We continue to shape our personality all our life. If we knew ourselves perfectly, we should die.
-Albert Camus

Man's main task in life is to give birth to himself, to become what he potentially is. The most important product of his effort is his own personality.
-Erich Fromm

Today, take a moment and ponder on your personality. How do you handle conflict? What is your reaction to betrayal? Understand, your personality has a lot to do with your perspective. Your perspective affects your vision, and your vision ultimately determines your destiny. Personality is very important. Take a few moments and ask yourself some questions, here are some examples:

Am I introverted or extroverted?
How do I handle pressure?
What happens when I get mad or upset?
How do I handle disappointment?
What is the health of my personality?

Scripture Reading:
1 Timothy 4, Matthew 9:4-14, 1 Samuel 30:1-11

ACTIVATION

Today, your prophetic assignment is to discover your personality type. Take a moment and find a personality type test, the internet is loaded with them. Some are accurate, others are not, but all will give you some sense of your personality type. Take a few moments today and take a personality quiz. This is your assignment.

Notes

Day 27

💡 INSPIRATION

Man is a spirit, who lives in a body, and possesses a soul. When God created Adam, He created Adam in His likeness and image (**Gen. 1:26-28**). God is trifold: Father, Son, and Holy Spirit. Man is trifold: spirit, soul, and body (**1 Thess. 5:23**). When we begin to deal with the personality, we must address the soul. Within your soul, you have three distinct functions and or compartments: the will, the mind, and the emotions. Now where all three of these different compartments intersect, that is called your personality. Your personality is where your will, mind, and emotions overlap.

And the LORD God formed man of the dust of the ground, and breathed into his nostrils the breath of life; and man became a living soul. (**Gen. 2:7**)

The word "soul" in the Hebrew is the word *nephesh*. Adam was a living soul. This literally means that Adam is now an animate object. Adam was ALIVE. When God created Adam, Adam was spirit. In Genesis, chapter 2, He formed Adam's body. When God breathed Adam's spirit into Adam's body, something supernatural happened. The soul was form. The soul is part earth, and part spirit. The soul is your negotiation faculty. Your soul is the liaison between your spirit and your body. The soul houses our will, mind, and emotions, which are all shaped throughout our life.

Life can deal us some very devastating blows. As we go through traumatic and dramatic events in our life, it shapes our soul. The soul is malleable and as we face life's pressures, it is squeezed and formed. This is why the Word of God is so important.

The law of the LORD is perfect, converting the soul: the testimony of the LORD is sure , making wise the simple. (**Psalm 19:11**)

This is most possibly my favorite verse in scripture. When it says the "law of the Lord", it is referring to the Word of God. The Word of God is law, because our God is a King. In the realm of royalty, anything the King speaks becomes law. God never gives suggestions. When God speaks, He commands. The soul is the negotiator and navigator between the spirit and the body. The Word of God is spirit and life according to John, chapter 6. When God speaks a word, He speaks it to your spirit. In order for that word to manifest, it has to be revealed through your physical body. In order to manifest a word, that word must go through your soul. So the Word of God is sown into your spirit, it must pass through your soul, so it can manifest in your body. This is what I call, the *Process of Translation*. The difficult reality of this process is understanding that because of our soul, much is lost in translation. Your soul is your filter, which has been shaped by your education, association, and socialization. This is called your paradigm. Your paradigm is the totality of your thinking system. It doesn't matter what promise is over your life, if your SOUL can't receive it, you will never have it. God wants to grip your soul. God wants to deal with your soul. As the Word of God passes through your soul to manifest in your body, it converts the soul. Every time the Word of God passes through your soul, all the dents, fragments, impacts, and imprints of the world are removed.

I beseech you therefore, brethren, by the mercies of God, that ye present your bodies a living sacrifice, holy, acceptable unto God, which is your reasonable service. 2 And be not conformed to this world: but be ye transformed by the renewing of your mind, that ye may prove what is that good, and acceptable, and perfect, will of God. (**Romans 12:1-2**)

MEDITATION

Today's meditation is designed to take your soul through bootcamp. Instead of a quote or concept today, you just have a scripture reading, but it is lengthy. Today a few moments to ponder on the transforming power of the Word of God.

Scripture Reading: **Psalm 119**

ACTIVATION

Today's prophetic exercise is a spiritual mapping exercise. Today we are begin to discover your personality according to the Word of God.

1. What is your favorite book of the Bible? (Choose 3)
2. What is your favorite scripture in the Bible? (Choose 2)
3. What are your favorite themes in the Bible? (Choose 3)
4. Who are your favorite Biblical characters? (Choose 3)
5. Name your favorite Biblical event. (Name 5)

Notes

_____
_____
_____
_____
_____
_____
_____
_____
_____
_____

Day 28

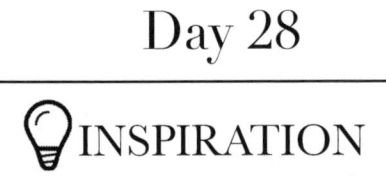

💡 INSPIRATION

Every dimension of man needs development. Man is a multidimensional being, having several compartments that all require specialized attention. Your finances need development. Your gift needs development. Everything requires development, even your personality. When our personalities don't receive the exposure they need, they never fully develop. Putting the pressures of life on the back of an underdeveloped personality is very dangerous. A solid, stable, successful personality is called maturity.

And saying, Repent ye : for the kingdom of heaven is at hand. (**Matt. 3:2**)

Every significant event in our life is shaping our perspective. This perspective is called your paradigm. A paradigm is formulated by one's education, association, and socialization. Your paradigm is how you see the world. When John, the Immerser, came preaching in the Wilderness of Judea, he came saying "Repent, for the Kingdom of Heaven is at hand" (Matt. 3:2). When John arrives on the scene, he is preaching a message about repentance. Repentance is not just saying, "I am sorry." Repentance is more than that. Repentance is not just feeling convicted of sin, it is more than that. Repentance is changing the way you see things. Repentance is the renovation of your perspective. Repentance is the reshaping of your paradigm. The word repentance is the Greek word *metanoeo*, and it denotes restoration or returning. To repent literally means to turn. When you repent, you are approaching a major adjustment. Whenever God begins to deal with your current perspective, it's because He is about to change your current position.

And the LORD God called unto Adam, and said unto him, Where art thou? (**Gen. 3:9**)

After Adam and Eve sinned, they hid. The scripture says that God found them hiding behind trees. How can you have the right perspective, when there is something obscuring your view. What is obscuring your view? Is it sin, pride, poverty, or perversion? What lenses do you use to view the world? Some people's personality is optimistic, others are pessimistic. It's all a matter of perspective. An immature perspective sees everything as a problem. A mature perspective can look at any situation and see a solution.

And why beholdest thou the mote that is in thy brother's eye, but considerest not the beam that is in thine own eye? (**Matt. 7:3**)

Immature people can only see the wrong in people. It takes a mature person to be able to look beyond a person's weaknesses and mistakes and say "you are still valuable." One's maturity is revealed by how they see others. One of the greatest weapons used against raising up new gift is dealing with comparison. As a gift begins to emerge, it looks for familiarity to stabilize. Whenever you begin to experience promotion, your surroundings begin to look different, and you'll find yourself blessed but uncomfortable. Some of you reading this right now are blessed, but uncomfortable. You must learn to love being uncomfortable. Your blessing is surrounded by your worst fear. Your destiny is disguised as a dilemma. You must change your perspective. In order to alter your perspective, you must amend your personality. God wants you to address your attitude, your tone of voice, your facial expressions, your perspective, your posture, your demeanor . . . God wants to address your personality!

MEDITATION

"We can complain because rose bushes have thorns, or rejoice because thorn bushes have roses."
-Abraham Lincoln

"There are no facts, only interpretations."
-Friedrich Nietzsche

Today, don't just ponder, but address your attitude and perspective. Every dimension of man needs development, even the personality. Today address the weaknesses in your personality. Take a few moments and ponder on times where your attitude may have closed a door for you. This may take an objective view. See Today's Prophetic Exercise.

Scripture Reading:
Genesis 3:4-14, Matthew 3, Matthew 7:18

ACTIVATION

Today's prophetic exercise is going to take vulnerability and honesty. Your assignment is to do an attitude assessment. Get someone you can trust, a notepad, and a pencil. Ask the person that you chose, being completely honest, to make a list of all the things they think you should change about yourself. Now this doesn't mean they're right, nor does this mean that you have to take their suggestion. This exercise is designed to build up your immune system to criticism. Destiny is surrounded by critics. Get use to it!

Day 29

💡 INSPIRATION

Personality is defined as the combination of characteristics or qualities that form an individual's distinctive character. Your personality is what makes you unique. When we begin to look at the personality, we must address both countenance and stature. Today we will deal with our countenance, and tomorrow we will conclude this session with the dynamics of stature.

Moreover when ye fast , be not, as the hypocrites, of a sad countenance: for they disfigure their faces, that they may appear unto men to fast . Verily I say unto you , They have their reward. (**Matthew 6:16**)

Throughout the scriptures, there are several different words used for countenance. In this scripture, the writer connects the word countenance with the subject's facial expression. Why is this important? What would you say if I said that God cared about your appearance? What would you say if I said God cares about your attitude and your facial expressions? God cares about our every detail. God cares about what makes you smile. God cares about what makes you happy. Your fears are interesting to God. Your desires, aspirations, and even issues are very important to God.

But the LORD said unto Samuel, Look not on his countenance, or on the height of his stature; because I have refused him: for the LORD seeth not as man seeth ; for man looketh on the outward appearance, but the LORD looketh on the heart. (**1 Sam. 16:7**)

While it is true that God doesn't consider the outward appearance, when it comes to choosing people for purpose, how you look is still important to God. Our facial expressions reveal much about our character, attitude, and disposition. Many times we use this scripture to justify a lack of excellence in our physical appearance, but it is clear through scripture that God cares about our appearance:

1. When Adam and Eve sinned, God clothed them (Gen. 3)
2. When Isaac was searching for a wife, precious raiment was one of the gifts (Gen. 24)
3. Jacob went to great lengths to make Joseph a fine coat of color (Gen. 37)
4. When the Priesthood was initiated, God used jewels to cover the Priest (Ex. 25)

Throughout the scripture we are introduced to a God who cares about appearance. Now understand, God knows your heart. God is neither confused, nor ignorant, when it comes to your body language. The face is the projector of the body. It is your face that reveals what's in your heart. Now most of us have mastered keeping our faces under control. No one ever knows what we are thinking, or how we are feeling. But your face is the projector of your personality. Our faces say a lot about how we feel, what we believe, and the level of our maturity. Have you ever said something to someone just to see their countenance fall? Have you ever seen the look of disappointment on a child's face? It is heart breaking.

For God, who commanded the light to shine out of darkness, hath shined in our hearts, to give the light of the knowledge of the glory of God in the face of Jesus Christ. (**2 Cor. 4:6**)

Say this with me! The Glory of God is seen in the Face of Jesus (repeat 3 times aloud). Our faces reveal our thoughts and feelings. The word glory here means essence or total presence. Jesus was the glory of God. Jesus was the face of God. When we are sad, we frown. When we are happy we smile. When we are confused, we look discombobulated. Our faces usually reveal how we feel. Can you imagine Adam's responsibility? Adam, having the responsibility of representing God to creation, had to be very careful of his body language. The smallest misstep or haphazard move could negatively and erroneously instruct the Earth on the nature of God. What if Adam had an attitude? All of creation would think God is mad when He is really happy. How has your lack of attention to your body language miscommunicated the plan and purpose of God? Growing in our calling requires us to address our personality.

And when Aaron and all the children of Israel saw Moses, behold, the skin of his face shone; and they were afraid to come nigh him. (**Ex. 34:30**)

And the children of Israel saw the face of Moses, that the skin of Moses' face shone : and Moses put the vail upon his face again, until he went in to speak with him. (**Ex. 34:35**)

When Moses came down from the top of the mountain, his facial expression revealed he had been with God. Moses, after his encounter with God, came down to the base of the mountain with his face shinning. This is a principle. Your face reveals your company. Your face reveals your attitude. Your face reveals your disposition. Maturity cares about how people perceive them. Let's be diligent to represent God and His amazing love and grace by our countenance.

MEDITATION

The face is a picture of the mind with the eyes as its interpreter.
-Cicero

A mask tells us more than a face.
-Oscar Wilde

Take a moment and ponder this thought: What does God's face look like when He looks at me? This is a very important question. The way you view God's face towards you will ultimately determine how you think God feels about you. Take a moment and meditate on God's face. Is He smiling? Is He upset? Do you think He is confused by some of your recent actions? I have a secret to tell you. God never stops smiling at you. God is irrevocably and eternally proud of you. Take a moment and think about how freeing that is.

Scripture Reading:
Exodus 34:25-35, 2 Corinthians 4:1-11, 1 Samuel 16:2-12

ACTIVATION

Today your prophetic exercise is to create a picture portfolio of your facial expression. Here are a list of expressions. Take a list of your face for each one, and create a portfolio. This can be used in relationships, leadership, and body language games to test your friends and family's knowledge of you. Here are the emotions:

1. Fear
2. Anger
3. Sadness
4. Joy
5. Disgust

6. Trust
7. Anticipation
8. Surprise

Notes

Day 30

💡 INSPIRATION

Today we conclude our session on personality with a study in authenticity. When we begin to address the personality, it is for the purpose of identification and articulation. At some point your anointing must be articulated. It's not just enough to know that you are anointed, you must know what you are anointed for, and who you are called to.

But he answered and said, I am not sent but unto the lost sheep of the house of Israel. (Matthew 15:24)

Jesus not only knew that He was anointed, but He had a clear understanding of who He was called to. Your assignment has specifics. Who are you called to? Who is your targeted audience? For every voice there is a people. For every people there is a voice. For every gift there is a time, and for every time there is a gift. Jesus said it like this,

And when he putteth forth his own sheep, he goeth before them, and the sheep follow him: for they know his voice. 5 And a stranger will they not follow, but will flee from him: for they know not the voice of strangers. (John 10:4-5)

Jesus was convinced that His voice belonged to a certain time, and a certain people. Have you ever asked God who you were called to? If not, pray this prayer aloud:

Father, in the name of Jesus, reveal the specifics of my creation, calling, and consecration. I want to be in your perfect will. Father, I ask that you lead, guide, and direct me into my active zones of ministry, never allowing me to waste my time, energy, anointing, or money. Father, reveal those who have been calibrated to my voice and anointing. Give me the tongue of the learned, so that as I speak, those connected to my voice would follow. Father I ask, like Mary the Mother of Jesus, that you give me quickening power, that even my salutation will prompt destiny in the people that hear my voice. Father, I thank you that you always hear me, it's in Jesus' name we pray, Amen.

Authenticity is about being uniquely you. Now that may seem easy, but in a world that celebrates duplicates, it can be very challenging. Most people are trying to escape their life, and be someone else. The anointing only reaches its full potential, when its carrier is authentic. When the anointing is held by a copycat, it loses its power by being constantly compared. Anointings are specific. The worse thing you can do is copy someone else's calling. You must discover what it is YOU are called to do.

Authenticity is defined as being genuine, special, and one of a kind. When God called you, He called YOU. God doesn't want you devaluing the anointing on your life. Authenticity must be celebrated. How are you different? What is unique about your personality. God doesn't want you to change as a person, but He wants to overshadow your humanity until you are changed into a different man. There is a certain power that is released when your identity is articulated. This is the function of fathers, to reveal the identity of the son.

And lo a voice from heaven, saying, This is my beloved Son, in whom I am well pleased. (Matthew 3:17)

Notice that it was the Father that articulated the Son's assignment. This is why Fathers are so important in ministry. Without Fathers, sons walk blindly, never truly coming into the specifics of their assignment. Fathers create a template for sons to follow, it is called a blueprint. Everyone needs a model for ministry, but impartation must come as a result of covenant, not by being a fan. Have you ever been guilty of copying someone in ministry? Who do you copy your style of prayer from? Who is your favorite preacher? These questions may seem juvenile, but they are actually great windows that you can use to peer into your personality.

MEDITATION

Concept: The Voice of God (Psalm 29)

Did you know that every voice has a distinct vibration? The same way your finger has a fingerprint, your voice has a voiceprint. Your voiceprint is the uniqueness and authenticity found in your pitch, tone, cadence, etc. You are unique. Do not forfeit your anointing by trying to sound like someone else. There is power in your voice. The voice of the Lord demonstrates this for us.

And his feet like unto fine brass, as if they burned in a furnace; and his voice as the sound of many waters. (Rev. 1:15)

Do you see that? God's voice is like the sound of many waters. This not only signifies the power of His voice to break through the dams and obstructions in our life, but His voice is also soothing. Have you ever been to a beach? Have you ever stood under a waterfall? Water can crash, but it can also trickle. God's voice has the ability to comfort us in unfamiliar places. Take a few moments and ponder on the voice of the Lord. Have you ever heard God audibly? Would you like to? Take a moment and ask to hear God's voice in a new way.

Scripture Reading:

Psalm 29, Matthew 3:12-17, John 10:1-10

ACTIVATION

Today's prophetic exercise is one that will train your hearing. This prophetic exercise can be done daily. Take a moment and find a quiet place. Make sure you have your journal and something to write with. Take the first 5 minutes to just ask God questions, please make sure you write the questions down. After you ask a question, take a few moments to listen in silence. Spend some quality time with the Lord until He answers all of your questions. Do not be timid. God is not afraid of you asking Him hard questions.

Notes

Session Seven: Price

Day 31

💡 INSPIRATION

How much are you willing to spend for greatness? How much would you sacrifice to be in God's will? How much does greatness cost? Today we begin session seven, Price. Every purpose has a price. All power has a price. Ministry is not for the weak at heart, nor is it for the faint. Ministry is serious business. We have seen many people jump into ministry excited, just to quit with only an ounce of sanity left. During this session we will explore the depth of your commitment. How far are you really willing to go? Is ministry just a cute idea to you?

For which of you, intending to build a tower, sitteth not down first, and counteth the cost, whether he have sufficient to finish it? (Luke 14:28)

Ministry isn't cheap. The word "cost" here literally means expense. Expense is defined as the cost required for something; the money spent on something. Ministry eats up the stingy and spits them out. Ministry requires you to be selfless. The first thing you must be willing to give up in ministry is . . . YOU! The price of ministry is great, especially if you do it right. God is not looking for part time employees!

Ministry isn't free, it costs you everything. Does ministry look easy to you? If ministry is appealing to you, it's because you're not looking at real ministry. Real ministry is nasty and messy. There is nothing about real ministry that is attractive. We have a generation of ministers that have formulated their idea of ministry based on television preachers. Real ministry is not in front of cameras, it is in the secrecy of darkness.

And certain women, which had been healed of evil spirits and infirmities, Mary called Magdalene, out of whom went seven devils (Luke 8:2)

We all remember Mary Magdalene. She was caught in the act of adultery and brought to Jesus to see what He would do. Jesus didn't condemn her, nor did Jesus embarrass her, Jesus covered her. This is real ministry. After Jesus covered her, Mary became a disciple of Jesus. The scripture is clear that after their initial encounter, Jesus cast out seven more devils. Notice that ministry didn't end with their first meeting, it only began. Ministry doesn't happen overnight, and rarely happens at all during preaching. Ministry is hands on. Ministry requires that you get dirty. Ministry requires a lack of sleep. Ministry requires great sacrifice. Luke, chapter 8 and verse 2, is such a powerful scripture. It lets us know that ministry isn't quick. Ministry takes time. Authentic ministry goes beyond the lights, stage, and audience . . . Real ministry happens behind closed doors.

And he that taketh not his cross, and followeth after me, is not worthy of me. (Matthew 10:38)

MEDITATION

A man who was completely innocent, offered himself as a sacrifice for the good of others, including his enemies, and became the ransom of the world. It was a perfect act. **-Mahatma Gandhi**

Great achievement is usually born of great sacrifice, and is never the result of selfishness. **-Napoleon Hill**

Human progress is neither automatic nor inevitable . . . Every step toward the goal of justice requires sacrifice, suffering, and struggle; the tireless exertions and passionate concern of dedicated individuals. **-Martin Luther King Jr.**

Take a moment and ponder on the things you've given up for ministry. We have all sacrificed something to do what God has called us to do. Can you think of any specific situation where you sacrificed a friendship or job for ministry? Take a few moments and write down some instances where sacrifice was inevitable.

Scripture Reading:
Matthew 10:33-42, Luke 14:23-33

ACTIVATION

Today's prophetic exercise is one of investment. Today you are to invest in someone else. This is a ministry exercise. Whether it be a Bible, study book, or anything pertaining to ministry, buy something for someone else that deals with ministry. Be specific, original, and thoughtful. Today you need to spend some money. Ministry is all about sacrifice. Today, I don't want you to be cheap. Impact someone's life with your sacrifice.

Notes
_____
_____
_____
_____
_____
_____

Day 32

💡 INSPIRATION

Price is not all about HOW MUCH, sometimes price is about HOW LONG. We don't place heavy emphasis on HOW LONG, but this is an important facet of your development. We live in a generation where most Christians do not have church homes. Most Believers wander from House to House, raiding the refrigerator, never making a commitment to build the House. I have found that when you are desperate for God to do something in your life, you don't care how long it takes. The scripture is filled with countless people who didn't receive their miracle when they expected it, but they were faithful.

Faithfulness is power. People with faithfulness are people with great attendance, why? Because faithful people have put in too much work to miss out on God doing anything. Faithful people understand the importance of attendance. How is your attendance at your local church? How often are you absent? People with faithfulness are punctual people. Faithfulness doesn't just say "BE THERE", but it says with a resounding voice, "BE THERE ON TIME." Commitment goes beyond signing up. Commitment must be there when the excitement wears off. Our generation believes that when the excitement wears off, it's time to leave. But it's quite the contrary, in fact your work doesn't begin until the fun is gone.

And Jacob served seven years for Rachel; and they seemed unto him but a few days, for the love he had to her. (Gen. 29:20)

This verse is loaded with prophetic principles. Notice first that Jacob worked seven years for his wife. Now if you know the whole story, this was just the beginning. Jacob ended up working a total of 14 years for the wife he wanted. How long are you willing to serve in your local assembly? What is your time limit? **The time limit of your service determines the potency of the promise. How long are you willing to serve?** I want to challenge your commitment. If revival is going to come to a city, a family, or a generation, it is going to take committed people. People that can see pass the hype, put their hand to the plow, and not look back. Babies continually ask, "are we there yet?" We need a generation that doesn't stop serving until the JOB IS DONE!

And let us not be weary in well doing : for in due season we shall reap, if we faint not. (Gal. 6:9)

Don't quit before you get blessed. Don't leave until your promise manifests. Don't walk away before your new day arrives. There is a divine blessing in faithfulness. Now faithfulness is not easy. As a matter of fact, it is not real faithfulness until you reach your "last nerve." Until you feel like quitting, you haven't begun. Are you a quitter? How often do you contemplate giving up? These are significant questions that you must answer. I have found that many people don't have faithfulness in them. They hate authority, they despise accountability, and they believe that they can make it in the Kingdom of God by themselves. They don't see the need for pastors. They don't support the local church with their finances. There are some people who are enemies to faithfulness. Be careful surrounding yourself with people who are FAITHLESS. Be careful spending time with people that don't understand the power of commitment. THEY WILL INFECT YOU (1 Cor. 15:33).

Make a pledge today to be committed to your local house. Let your dedication be measured in decades, not years. Allow the Lord to grow your inheritance. Commit to the vision of the House. Commit to your Senior Pastor and Leaders. Commit to revival and transformation. Today we all make a commitment to remain faithful to the assignment God has given us corporately. Commit to perfect attendance. Commit to showing up early and leaving late. Commit to doing more than your peers. Show everyone how dedicated and determined you are to BUILD THE HOUSE! Can you say this prayer with me aloud:

Father, address every ounce of inconsistency in my service. I want to be faithful. Father, I am a faithful tither. I am a faithful server. I am a faithful member. Father increase my faithfulness. I ask that you anoint my hands to work without getting tired. Expand my endurance and increase my stamina to serve. I want to make you proud. Father, let my faithfulness be a token of your goodness and mercy. Father, let my faithfulness reveal what an amazing God you are in my generation. Utilize my members for faithfulness. Utilize my mind for faithfulness. I commit to a life of service and humility. In Jesus' name, Amen.

MEDITATION

Concept: The Local Church (Matthew 16:18, Hebrews 10:25)

The scripture is clear that the church is a mystery whose function can only be revealed by the Holy Spirit. The church will not make sense to you unless you are spiritual. In Matthew 16, Jesus uses a word we have never seen before, "church". Now this word was common in Jesus' day and time. The word church is the Greek word *ecclesia,* and it literally means a called out group of people. In the times of Jesus, this word was used for the senate to denote a governing body. The church is the senate of Heaven. The church is made up of people God has called out of the world, to rule on His behalf. Are you apart of a local church? What do you do? Where do you serve? How many hours a week do you dedicate? The local church is only as powerful as the Believers that attend.

Take a moment and ponder on the beauty of the Church. Did you know Jesus died for the church? YES! I doubt Jesus would appreciate us being unfaithful to something He died for. Jesus gave His life for the Church. The church of Jesus Christ is an amazing phenomenon. That God could call a group of sinners, transform them, and then use them to direct Kingdom affairs. Can you take a few moments and just praise God audibly for His grace? No seriously, do it now... I will wait. (Praise Break)

Scripture Reading:
Gen. 29:15-25, Galatians 6:4-14, Matthew 16:13-23

ACTIVATION

Today your prophetic assignment is an exercise of commitment. Today your assignment is to commit to a month of faithful service. You will attend every meeting, service, recreational event, and fellowship. WE ARE ABOUT TO SHIFT GEARS. Your assignment is to renew your commitment to your local church. Find a creative way to display your level of commitment to your local assembly.

Notes

_____
_____
_____
_____
_____
_____

Day 33

💡 INSPIRATION

We have dealt with HOW MUCH and HOW LONG, but today we venture into the world of HOW FAR. Price is not always about how much something is, or even how long it takes to get it, people who want something bad enough are willing to go to great lengths to fulfill their dreams and conquer their goals. How far are you willing to go? This is a question of mental fortitude. This is a question of will power. I have heard of people driving great distances, even flying, to go to their favorite restaurant and get their favorite dish. When you really want something you are willing to travel miles to get it. What is the furthest distance you've travelled for something you desired?

And David longed, and said, Oh that one would give me drink of the water of the well of Bethlehem, which is by the gate! (2 Sam. 23:15)

We all know David. David was an extreme guy. His personality was large, and he was known to have a temper. David had an insatiable hunger for the presence of God, and his priority was the glory. But just like us, David had his guilty pleasures. David had developed a taste for water that came from a specific well in Bethlehem. The problem with this is, the well was located behind enemy lines. The Philistines had seized and captured Bethlehem, and now controlled it's borders. When David cries out for a drink, the scripture says that his men went to work. How far are you willing to go? Ministry is not about the limelight. Ministry is not about being seen. Ministry is about sacrifice. The price of ministry is great for us all. Some pay with their sanity, others with their family . . . some pay the price of ministry with their youth, or health, but we all pay a price. Ministry isn't easy, it's not designed to be.

And the three mighty men brake through the host of the Philistines, and drew water out of the well of Bethlehem, that was by the gate, and took it, and brought it to David: nevertheless he would not drink thereof, but poured it out unto the LORD. (2 Sam. 23:15)

After David asked for a drink of water from this dangerous place, his men got up and went into action. Every Elijah, needs an Elisha. Every Moses, needs a Joshua. Every Paul needs a Timothy. And every David, needs mighty men. The words "mighty men" denote strength in physicality, mental aptitude, character, gift and, skill. These men had spent time preparing, practicing, and planning. How far are you willing to go? What does your assignment call for? Does it call for you running through a troop of Philistines to get a glass of water? How far are you willing to go? Distance determines dedication. You can not say that you are dedicated to something, if you are not willing to go the distance. How far do you travel for church? How far do you travel for work? How far do you travel for recreation? The sad truth is people will travel hours to go shopping, and not twenty minutes to worship the King of Kings. How far are you willing to go?

This story has always intrigued me. The dedication of these men are incredible. If you had to measure your dedication to your Pastor, Church, and Assignment by these men, how would you measure up? These men were willing to die to quench the thirst of their David. Yes, their David. There comes a point in service where you take responsibility for your leaders. This is the place God is calling you to. You are a watchman, you are a prophetic guard, you are personal intercessors to your leaders. God is increasing the burden you have for your leaders. The scripture says that these "mighty men" broke through the host of the Philistines. The HOW FAR of ministry takes breakthrough power. It takes the ability to find your second wind, because fatigue can always set in. But we decree fresh winds are blowing, and you are being rejuvenated.

But they that wait upon the LORD shall renew their strength; they shall mount up with wings as eagles; they shall run, and not be weary; and they shall walk, and not faint. (Isa. 40:31)

MEDITATION

Concept: Armor Bearers (1 Sam. 17:7)

The difference between a successful person is not a lack of strength, not a lack of knowledge, but rather a lack of will. **-Vincent Lombardi**

It says of Goliath, that one went out in front of him carrying his shield. This was Goliath's armor bearer. In the Old Testament there were three classifications of priests: the levites, the priests, and then the High Priest. The levites were temple workers, who usually resided in the outer court and handled the manual and physical tasks of ministry. They carried the sacrifices, washed all the utensils, and cleaned up after worship. An armor bearer is one who has been given responsibility to care for another. An armor bearer is an aid. An armor bearer is help. Maybe you feel like God is calling you to carry the weight of your leader, here are a few questions to ask first:

1. What is my level of selfishness?
2. Where does my immaturity show up?
3. Do I have the capacity to constantly put someone before me?
4. How do I react when people "treat me" like a servant?
5. Am I ok being looked over?
6. How do I allow my personal life to affect my service?
7. Do I truly have a servant's heart?

Take a few moments and ponder these questions. Spend a few minutes on each. Repeat these questions both internally and aloud. Allow the Holy Spirit to minister to you through these questions.

Scripture Reading:
2 Samuel 23

ACTIVATION

Todays prophetic exercise is designed to challenge your stamina in service. Serving takes endurance. Today is the day you step into the place of a watchmen. I want you to find an area of service or something special that **ONLY YOU** can do for your leader(s), and do it consistently. Find an area of service that you can be dedicated to. This should go beyond corporate ministry, and touch your leader in a personal area.

Notes

_____
_____
_____
_____
_____
_____
_____
_____
_____
_____
_____
_____
_____
_____

Day 34

💡 INSPIRATION

Whenever we deal with concepts like price, we must address value. Value is how much a thing is worth. Value can be both objective, and subjective. A bottle of expensive water, because of how it's filtered, and where it comes from, could cost you up to ten dollars. But the glass of water that David's Mighty men retrieved from Bethlehem in 2nd Samuel, chapter 23 . . . priceless. Some things are so valuable, you cannot attach a price to them. There are certain things that diminish in rank when you put a price tag on it: people, anointings, things with sentimental force, the next generation, and moments, just to name a few.

The currency of ministry is moments. Divine encounters, supernatural experiences, accelerated favor, all of these produce the moments we need for transformation. It's these moments that we live for. To be in the presence of the King, this is what we long for. But presence, comes with a price. How do you weigh your moments and/or encounters with the Lord? How do you measure transformation?

Forasmuch as ye know that ye were not redeemed with corruptible things, as silver and gold, from your vain conversation received by tradition from your fathers; 19 But with the precious blood of Christ, as of a lamb without blemish and without spot: (1 Peter 1:18-19)

When it came to purchasing you, God wasn't cheap. How much someone is willing to pay for a thing, reveals it's value. The scripture says that God didn't use minerals, silver or gold, to redeem us, but

God used BLOOD! Not just any blood, His own blood. How much are you worth that the God of the universe would come and die for you? Now if that doesn't excite you, maybe this will. The powerful thing about Jesus dying for our sins, is that He did it with full knowledge of all of your weaknesses. Jesus didn't die for you because you were worthy. Jesus' death made you worthy. Regardless of how much you were worth before, you could have been through a divorce, you could have been molested and abused, but regardless of your past, God says "they're mine, and they're not cheap!" Jesus solidified your value . . . PRICELESS.

The word used to describe Jesus' blood is the word "precious." This word literally is a word of value. The word "precious" means to be held in high honor, great esteem, something expensive, as with great price. Always remember that demons are cheap. Satan is cheap. Sin is cheap. Have you ever bought a cheap car? Have you ever purchased cheap clothes? Some of you are bound by cheap friends. Cheap friends are the most expensive kind of friends to have. SELAH! Cheap things look good for a moment, just to break down tomorrow. Cheap things cover you, but they cause rashes. Cheap things twinkle, but can't reflect real light like diamonds. Are you cheap? How much are you willing to spend to be all you can be?

MEDITATION

Concept: Ransom (1 Tim. 2:6)
Who gave himself a ransom for all, to be testified in due time. (1 Tim. 2:6)

After Adam, by nature of his treason, forfeited our rights and power to Satan, Jesus came to redeem what Adam lost. Concepts like redemption and ransom run throughout the Bible. Prophets like Hosea deal with these themes in such a dramatic way. Hosea was instructed by God to marry a prostitute to demonstrate Israel's lack of faithfulness to covenant. After Hosea obeyed God, his wife- the harlot- still walks the streets at night looking for her past. Well one day when she goes out, she doesn't come back.

Then said the LORD unto me, Go yet, love a woman beloved of her friend, yet an adulteress, according to the love of the LORD toward the children of Israel, who look to other gods, and love flagons of wine. 2 So I bought her to me for fifteen pieces of silver, and for an homer of barley, and an half homer of barley: (Hosea 3:1-2)

When Hosea finds Gomer, he pays a "ransom" to get her back. This is the powerful story of redemption. Hosea was willing to pay for something he already owned. When you love something, you can't put a price tag on it. When you want something, regardless of how much it is, you're willing to pay for it. Ransom is defined as the sum of money or other payment demanded or paid for the release of a prisoner. Jesus paid your bond.

Take a moment and think about the times God has bailed you out of situations you put yourself into. Take a moment and worship our Father for the times He delivered you, and you didn't deserve it. Today, cultivate an attitude of thanksgiving by thinking about how Jesus ransomed you!

Scripture Reading:
Hosea 3, 1 Timothy 2:1-11, 1 Peter 1:13-23

ACTIVATION

Todays prophetic exercise is a challenge of your will, determination, focus, and honesty. Your assignment today is not to speak a negative word. Today you can not complain, get mad, upset, frown, sigh, murmur, or be reclusive. Today is the day you take control of your emotions. Your assignment today is to maintain an attitude of thanksgiving throughout the entire day. This is your assignment.

Notes

Day 35

💡 INSPIRATION

As we conclude session seven, we return to the subject of sacrifice. When we speak of price, we are actually speaking of sacrifice. Sacrifice is a gut-wrenching word. It engenders thoughts of pain, death, blood, screams, and tears, and rightfully so. Wherever there is sacrifice, there will be an altar. The word "altar" actually means the killing place, or the slaughter place. In the Days of Old, altars were erected to worship a deity. The people of God would establish an altar and burn offerings unto the Most High God, El Elyon. When God received the sacrifice, he did so by sending fire. Fire is always a sign of passion, heat, and love that enflames and engulfs. When the sacrifice was put on the altar, it was then tied down. Are you tied down to your church, or can you leave whenever you are ready? Are you tied down in your marriage, or can you leave whenever you are ready? Dedication is depicted by sacrifice. The quicker you can leave something reveals how committed you were in the first place.

I beseech you therefore, brethren, by the mercies of God, that ye present your bodies a living sacrifice, holy, acceptable unto God, which is your reasonable service. (Romans 12:1)

God doesn't want lambs and doves as offerings anymore, He wants you. We are the sacrifice that's been placed on the altar, tied down by His love. This is clearly seen in the story of Abraham and Isaac. Abraham was given a promise, that he would have a son, and it took almost a generation to see this promise come to pass. And after God blesses Abraham with his son, God speaks to Abraham and says, "Kill him!" WAIT A MINUTE! I can imagine Abraham pleading, "but this is what I've been waiting for my entire life for!" And God still says, without even blinking an eye, "KILL IT!" How could God ask that of you? How could a loving God ask you to kill your hopes and dreams? IT'S CALLED SACRIFICE! And if you want to be great, you and sacrifice must become best friends.

If any man come to me, and hate not his father, and mother, and wife, and children, and brethren, and sisters, yea, and his own life also, he cannot be my disciple. (Luke 14:26)

What a statement! Jesus wasn't playing games. What Jesus is dealing with here is sacrifice. The price of greatness is loneliness, and if that's too big a price, forfeit the fame. There is a price for everything. Jesus said that the price of being His disciple was to hate his family. Jesus wasn't speaking of literal hate, but levels of commitment. Jesus said, if you are going to be my disciple, I must be your first priority. WOW. And this wasn't written to singles, but to husbands and parents. As a parent, I have to be more committed to Jesus, than to my kids. Now you may ask, where is the balance? I have to be honest, I don't see "balance" in Jesus' statement, nor His ministry.

While he yet talked to the people, behold, his mother and his brethren stood without, desiring to speak with him. 47 Then one said unto him, Behold, thy mother and thy brethren stand without, desiring to speak with thee. 48 But he answered and said unto him that told him, Who is my mother? and who are my brethren? 49 And he stretched forth his hand toward his disciples, and said, Behold my mother and my brethren! 50 For whosoever shall do the will of my Father which is in heaven, the same is my brother, and sister, and mother. (Matthew 12:46-50)

While Jesus was sitting in a ministry strategy meeting, his family came to the door. You know how family can be, they want you to stop everything you're doing to care for them. But when they told Jesus that his mom was at the door, He replied, "who is my mom?" Jesus was a cold dude. Jesus then looked at His disciples, pointing at them, and said "you are my family." If this isn't your attitude, maybe ministry isn't for you. Maybe ministry is just a cute idea, but it can't be a calling. When ministry is a calling, everyone else must accommodate that burden. When ministry is a calling, even if you have 10 kids, you will find a way to worship and work at the same time. God is our highest calling. The price must be paid. How much are you willing to spend? How far are you willing to go? How much are you willing to take? What's your breaking point in service? WE ARE ABOUT TO SHIFT GEARS!

MEDITATION

A team will always appreciate a great individual if he's willing to sacrifice for the group. **-Kareem Abdul-Jabbar**

It takes tremendous will to compete in any athletic endeavor, so it meant going to bed early and getting my homework done in advance. I had to sacrifice things, like a social life, to be a skater at 15. But I loved skating so much that it was worth everything to me. **-Vera Wang**

These two quotes are by tremendous competitors that reached the peak of their performance and obtained some of the highest awards in sports. You don't get there without sacrifice. Today I want you to ponder on the beauty of sacrifice. You must convince your brain that sacrifice feels good. You must convince your brain that sacrifice is necessary. And you must address the spirit of self preservation. There is an innate instinct in all human beings called self preservation. Self preservation is when your will won't let you die or voluntarily get in harms way. That's why it is hard to hurt yourself intentionally.

And they overcame him by the blood of the Lamb, and by the word of their testimony; and they loved not their lives unto the death. (Rev. 12:11)

I love this passage of scripture. We quote this verse often, but usually miss the end of the verse. It says, "they loved not their lives unto the death." That literally means they were willing to die. If you aren't willing to die for it, you're wasting your time. You can't love your life more than you love Jesus. Take a moment and ponder on the beauty of sacrifice, and everything that Jesus did for us on the cross.

Scripture Reading:
Genesis 22, Romans 12

ACTIVATION

Today your assignment is to replace one of your meals with work. Either during breakfast, lunch, or dinner, dedicate time to helping someone else complete a task. This is your assignment.

Notes

_____
_____
_____
_____
_____
_____

THE JOURNEY

Session Eight: Presence

Day 36

💡 INSPIRATION

Welcome to the last session of The Journey, Presence. In this session we will explore the importance of presence and how the presence of God functions. Presence is a big deal within the Kingdom of God. When Jesus was crucified and buried, the disciples scattered and locked themselves behind closed doors. The man they had lived with for just shy of 3 years was now gone. We have all lost loved ones, but this was a little different. This was not a family member, this was not just a friend, this was our Master. The one who led and guided us with divine wisdom. Jesus was a walking Journey. Everywhere He went, He created adventures. These men didn't just love Jesus, the Messiah, they loved Jesus the man.

And the two disciples heard him speak, and they followed Jesus. 38 Then Jesus turned, and saw them following, and saith unto them, What seek ye? They said unto him, Rabbi, (which is to say, being interpreted, Master,) where dwellest thou? 39 He saith unto them, Come and see. They came and saw where he dwelt, and abode with him that day: for it was about the tenth hour. (John 1:37-39)

After this encounter with Jesus, they never left Him. Whatever they saw and experienced in Jesus' house demanded their loyalty forever. These men committed their lives to the Master. Everyday they walked with Him, ate with Him, ministered with Him, and now . . . He was gone. How broken they must have felt. How purposeless they had to feel. This man carried their destiny, and now He's gone. Have you ever missed someone so much that you longed for their presence? Maybe it was a friend that moved away, or a long distance relationship, but there are specific times in our lives when we long for presence. Presence is that feeling that someone else is in the room with you. God's presence is comforting, rejuvenating, peaceful, and powerful. There is no place like the presence of God. Can you say that with me? THERE IS NO PLACE LIKE YOUR PRESENCE GOD (repeat 3 times aloud).

When Jesus was taken captive in the Garden, and the disciples fled, that was the last time they felt His presence. Jesus would be tried, judged, sentenced, and executed all in a matter of hours. By the time the disciples knew what had happened to the Master, it was too late, He was gone. So for three days the disciples, shut up in a locked room, didn't have presence. Have you ever felt abandoned? Have you ever felt alone? This is what the disciples felt like for three days, absolute abandonment.

When Jesus was on the cross, He experienced this.

Now from the sixth hour there was darkness over all the land unto the ninth hour. 46 And about the ninth hour Jesus cried with a loud voice, saying , Eli, Eli, lama sabachthani? that is to say, My God, my God, why hast thou forsaken me? (Matthew 27:45-46)

As Jesus hung on the cross, the Father watched over Him. From the womb of Mary, to the Garden of Pressing, to now His final breath, God was watching. From the time Jesus, as a little boy, was teaching in the temple, until the time He was judged in the temple, the Father was watching. Jesus always knew His Father was watching. But now, in the darkest moment of His life, the Father is going to do something He has never done. The Father is going to turn His back on the Son. God can not look upon sin. And when Jesus was on the cross, He became sin (2 Cor. 5:21). Jesus knew that His Father had been with Him every step of His life, but now, getting ready to go to Hell, His Father had to turn away. Can you imagine, at the most

THE JOURNEY

difficult moment of your life, the support you've always had is no longer there. There is no one to shout, "GOOD JOB!" No one to encourage you when you get tired, and motivate you when you feel discouraged. Have you ever been there?

What Jesus did on the cross is nothing short of amazing. Jesus became sin. Jesus literally became every disgusting thing we struggle with, and there on the cross, God judged it. The wages of sin is death, and sin can not make it into the presence of God. So when Jesus died, He went to Hell. For three days the disciples are locked in a room with no presence. For three days Jesus is locked in Hell with no presence. "But on the third day", as the old Baptist preacher would say, "Early Sunday morning, He got up with all power in His hands." When Jesus got up from the grave, it was the greatest comeback in all of history. But the disciples were still hiding, afraid, and locked behind closed doors.

Then the same day at evening, being the first day of the week, when the doors were shut where the disciples were assembled for fear of the Jews, came Jesus and stood in the midst, and saith unto them, Peace be unto you. 20 And when he had so said, he shewed unto them his hands and his side. Then were the disciples glad, when they saw the Lord. 21 Then said Jesus to them again, Peace be unto you: as my Father hath sent me, even so send I you. 22 And when he had said this, he breathed on them, and saith unto them, Receive ye the Holy Ghost: (John 20:19-22)

Locked behind closed doors, the disciples trembled in fear. But guess what? Jesus can walk through closed doors! Jesus shows up, proving to them it was Him, and then proceeding to breathe on them the very *pneuma* of God. What Jesus was saying in essence was, "receive my presence, so you'll never be without me again." Jesus gave them something in that moment. Knowing the agonizing feeling of being alone, locked away, Jesus gave them His presence. It was the first thing that Jesus gave the disciples, the very presence of God. If this was the first thing that Jesus gave us after His resurrection, it must be of utmost importance. Jesus has made us a promise.

Let your conversation be without covetousness; and be content with such things as ye have : for he hath said , I will never leave thee, nor forsake thee. (Hebrews 13:5)

Jesus has made us a promise, that He'll never take His presence away from us again. Isn't that amazing. Our God is committed to never leaving us, even when we try to leave Him. Jesus said that He would be with us, even until the end of time (Matthew 28:20). Be encouraged today that God is with you. Be bold today, knowing that He is walking with you, and He always will.

MEDITATION

Concept: God's Omnipresence vs. Jesus

The concept of God's omnipresence is widely accepted and understood in the Christian world today. The concept of omnipresence states that God is everywhere at the same time. This is an important theological concept, because it forms our understanding of God's scope of covering. God is able to watch after you and me, at the same time, even if we are in different parts of the World. God is just as committed to me, as He is to you, so He made it so He could be in two places at once. God is everywhere. Now, this is not the same as the New Agers, who believe that God is IN everything, or represented BY everything. NO! This is foolishness. God created the tree, He is not in the tree. God created the bird, but He is not a bird. You can not reduce the Creator down to the creature. But God loved US so much that He humiliated Himself and became a man. He didn't become a bird or tree, He became just like me.

When Jesus came, He was not an offshoot of God's omnipresence. Jesus is the glory of God. Jesus is the smoke that filled the Holies of Holies. Jesus is the light of the Shekinah. Jesus is the manifest, tangible, presence of God. Jesus is the raw presence of Jehovah. Take a moment and ponder on the presence of God. What are some times where you felt abandoned by God? Are you mad at God? Have you ever felt forsaken by God? Take a moment a ponder on the importance of God's presence.

Scripture Reading:
John 1:34-44, Matthew 27:40-50, Psalm 139

ACTIVATION

Your prophetic assignment is to STOP what you are doing RIGHT NOW, lift your hands, open your mouth, regardless of where you are, and begin to worship Jesus right now. Don't stop until you feel His presence. Let's see how bold you are! Go!

Notes

_____
_____
_____
_____
_____
_____
_____
_____
_____
_____
_____

Day 37

💡 INSPIRATION

Leadership is usually measured in tangibles. Tangibles are qualities that can be measured, like physical strength, intelligence, skills, abilities, and talents. But within the world of greatness, there are also intangibles. Intangibles are qualities like confidence or responsibility. Intangibles can't be measured with a scientific instrument, nor can they be seen with the naked eye. Intangibles are usually discerned through the phrase, "there is just something different about them." Presence is considered an intangible. Since you can't see it, and since there is no instrument of measuring, presence is considered one of the intangibles of greatness. Great people carry great presence. When people with presence walk into a room, everyone knows they are there. Have you ever been to a church service or concert, and when the main event walked in the room, you could feel the energy? This is presence. Great people command attention, and this is what presence does. Presence captivates the attention of men, and without it, it is hard to command crowds. Jesus had presence. Another word for presence is stature.

And Jesus increased in wisdom and stature,a and in favour with God and man. (Luke 2:52)

Jesus increased in three areas: wisdom, stature, and in favor with both God and man. These three areas must be increased in our lives as well. As we increase in wisdom, we make better decisions. As we increase in favor, greater doors open. As we increase in stature, people's level of respect for you increases. Respect is important. Respect means to have due regard for the feelings, wishes, rights, or traditions of another. People with presence demand respect. This is why, when it came to God and His people, the presence was so important. Israel didn't have weapons, or armies, allies, or friends.

Israel was surrounded by nations that were stronger, more technologically advanced, better weaponry, and all Israel was given was presence.

Now therefore, I pray thee, if I have found grace in thy sight, shew me now thy way, that I may know thee, that I may find grace in thy sight: and consider that this nation is thy people. 14 And he said, My presence shall go with thee, and I will give thee rest. 15 And he said unto him, If thy presence go not with me, carry us not up hence. 16 For wherein shall it be known here that I and thy people have found grace in thy sight? is it not in that thou goest with us? so shall we be separated, I and thy people, from all the people that are upon the face of the earth. 17 And the LORD said unto Moses, I will do this thing also that thou hast spoken: for thou hast found grace in my sight, and I know thee by name. (Ex. 33:13-17)

Moses asked, "Lord what makes us different than all the other nations of the Earth?" This is a great question. Israel, as a nation, didn't have what other nations had. They didn't have a city, nor did they even have land. Israel had no legislative process, no cities, no army or military power, Israel didn't look much like a nation.

And ye shall be unto me a kingdom of priests, and an holy nation. These are the words which thou shalt speak unto the children of Israel. (Ex. 19:6)

God didn't make Israel like every other nation. For most nations, their prized possession is their population, or job creation rate. For most nations, their prized possession is the number of millionaires they produce, or the size of their military. Israel's prize was always God's presence. As the people of God, our confidence can't be in money, or family, education or jobs . . . it must be in the presence of the Lord.

Cast me not away from thy presence; and take not thy holy spirit from me. (Psalm 51:11)

David prayed this prayer with tears running down his face. David pleaded with God, "please do not take your presence from me." The presence of God is life. The presence of God is power. The presence of God is safety. Life literally flows from God's presence. This is why, if you don't frequently enter His presence, you will feel drained and empty of life. The presence of God is literally raw life. When was the last time that the presence of God was so tangible you could hardly stand? When was the last night you had an encounter in the presence of the Lord? The presence is the difference maker, are you ready for an encounter?

MEDITATION

Concept: Being Slain in the Spirit (2 Chron. 5:14, Rev. 1:17)

And for fear of him the keepers did shake , and became as dead men (Matthew 28:4)

If you have been in or around church for any length of time, you have probably heard the term "being slain in the spirit." This is usually most clearly seen when people are prayed for, and fall out under the power of God. Throughout the scripture we see at times where the presence of God, or a person, became so overwhelming that it caused people to fall as if they were dead. The word "slain" means to kill. Have you ever been in a church service and began to feel dizzy? Have you ever been worshipping God, and your knees became weak? When you feel this, do not fight it, God is trying to give you an experience. Many times God knocks us down, to prophetically pick us back up. We see this in the ordinance of baptism. The prophetic action of going down and coming up represents a new birth. When the power of God overwhelms you, and you yield to Him by falling, because it is a choice, God has the opportunity to move pass your intellect and work on your heart.

Take a moment and ponder on times where you were overwhelmed with God's presence? Have you ever fallen out in His presence? If not, why? Are you afraid of being embarrassed? Take a few moments and think on the times where you could have fallen, but you fought it.

Scripture Reading
Exodus 33:13-23, Psalm 51

ACTIVATION

Today your assignment is to find a public place to lay prostrate. You heard me right. WE JUST SHIFTED GEARS. Today, put your worship on public display. Find a public place and lay prostrate, or lift your hands as high as they can go for an extended period of time. Today your prophetic exercise is to make your God known publicly, by worshipping so everyone can see. This is your assignment!

Notes

_____
_____
_____
_____
_____
_____
_____

Day 38

💡 INSPIRATION

The presence of God is precious. The presence of God should never be taken lightly. Mature Believers understand the power of His presence. In most churches in America, the preaching of the word of God is the pinnacle of their experience. This should never be so. Why do we esteem the presence of a man, more than the presence of God? The greatest moment within a service, is the very presence of God. We must return to seeking His presence. Once the church, locally and globally, becomes addicted to His presence, our cities will change automatically. The presence of God has the ability to turn hearts, and convict sinners. Many times we get ourselves in trouble by trying to do the job of the Holy Spirit. It is not your job to convict sinners, your job is to love them. It is not your job to change people, that is the Holy Spirit's job. The presence can get the job done. The presence of God must be our priority. Most Believers are looking to get married, make money, and even finish school. All of these are noble aspiration, but nothing compares to being a presence seeker.

We all are familiar with Saul. Saul was the first king of Israel. He was chosen by the people, because they wanted a king like every other nation under Heaven. It is a dangerous thing when Believers long to live like the world. Saul was a handsome guy. The scripture says that he was head and shoulders above his peers. His was intelligent, witty, and a people person. Saul would seem to be the perfect king. But there was one problem, he didn't want God's presence. Before Saul ascended to the throne, the Ark of the Covenant was stolen in battle.

And the Philistines took the ark of God, and brought it from Ebenezer unto Ashdod. 2 When the Philistines took the ark of God, they brought it into the house of Dagon, and set it by Dagon. (1 Sam. 5:1-2)

When Saul comes to the throne, the Ark of God has been returned, but it has remained in Abinadab's house for 20 years. Not at one point does Saul ask, "where is the glory?" When you have leaders that care more about money than glory, a generation can be lost. When we have congregants that care more about the weather than the glory, we will have empty churches. I am pleading with you, go after the glory of God. We desperately need a glory generation. The rate of revival would increase if we all went after the glory of God.

During Saul's entire reign, the glory was only utilized once, and that was for war. Can you imagine how God feels when you only come to Him when you are in trouble? Have you ever had a friend that only called you when they needed money? How did that make you feel? During Saul's administration, the glory was an after thought. So God found a little shepherd boy. This boy had no pedigree. David wasn't the tallest, nor was he the most handsome. The scripture says that David was ruddy. This means David was rough around the edges. David was no supermodel, but he loved God with all his heart.

And when he had removed him, he raised up unto them David to be their king; to whom also he gave testimony, and said, I have found David the son of Jesse, a man after mine own heart, which shall fulfil all my will. (Acts 13:22)

David was a man after God's own heart. David wasn't after a microphone, and he didn't want to be the next big church sensation. David wanted the glory of God. The first thing David did when he ascended to the throne, was go after the glory. 2nd Samuel, chapter 6, details the journey David travelled to return the Ark of God to it's rightful place. How much presence is in your life? How much glory do you want? How much Jesus can you handle? Are you like Saul, someone who really doesn't care about the presence of God? Or, are you like David, and it's your top priority? The glory must return to our lives, families, churches, and communities. And guess what? You are going to bring it back. This is the purpose for which you were born, to be a glory carrier.

MEDITATION

Concept: The Ark of God (Ex. 25:10)

And they shall make an ark of shittim wood: two cubits and a half shall be the length thereof, and a cubit and a half the breadth thereof, and a cubit and a half the height thereof. 11 And thou shalt overlay it with pure gold, within and without shalt thou overlay it, and shalt make upon it a crown of gold round about. (Ex. 25:10-11)

There are a few arks mentioned in Scripture: the ark of Noah, Moses' ark, the ark of God, and the ark of Salvation, which is Jesus Christ. Throughout the Scripture you will notice that God always raised up an ark, or safe place, for His people. In Noah's day, the ark was made to deliver the righteous during the flood. In Moses' day, the ark was designed to protect Moses in a river filled with crocodiles. But in the Wilderness, Moses and his men, were commanded by God to build something different. The Ark of the Covenant was a wooden box, overlaid with gold, which contained some important artifacts: the stone tablets that contained the ten commandment, a golden pot of manna, and Aaron's rod that had budded. The Ark was not just another piece of furniture. It represented the Glory of God.

Take a moment and ponder on something you have that has sentimental value. What is something that you put extreme worth and value on. How would you feel if it was stolen? How would you feel if it was lost? How would you feel if someone, who didn't realize how important it was, treated it like trash? Take a moment and ponder on precious things, and ask yourself these questions:

1. What is important to me?
2. Why are these items important, and who gave them to me?
3. Do I put more emphasis on material possessions than I do on the presence of God?
4. What can I do to focus people's attention toward the Glory of God and not me?

Scripture Reading:
1 Samuel 4, 1 Samuel 5, John 1

ACTIVATION

Today's prophetic exercise is one designed to stretch your evangelistic capacity. Your assignment today is to lead someone to Christ. WE JUST SHIFTED GEARS. Today your job is to minister life to someone. Find someone, it can be a stranger or a family member that doesn't know Christ, or who has yet to accept Jesus into their life, and lead them in the Sinner's Prayer. Here is a version of the Sinner's Prayer that you can use:

Dear God in heaven, I come to you in the name of Jesus. I acknowledge to You that I am a sinner, and I am sorry for my sins and the life that I have lived; I need your forgiveness.

I believe that your only begotten Son Jesus Christ shed His precious blood on the cross at Calvary and died for my sins, and I am now willing to turn from my sin.

You said in Your Holy Word, Romans 10:9 that if we confess the Lord our God and believe in our hearts that God raised Jesus from the dead, we shall be saved.

Right now I confess Jesus as the Lord of my soul. With my heart, I believe that God raised Jesus from the dead. This very moment I accept Jesus Christ as my own personal Savior and according to His Word, right now I am saved.

Thank you Jesus for dying for me and giving me eternal life.
Amen.

Notes

Day 39

💡 INSPIRATION

There are some people that go after power, some after popularity, but our desire is for the presence of God. Being a presence seeker is the greatest honor in the world. Being a God chaser is the highest honor in all the Earth. It is a privilege to go after the Lord of Lords. God loves being chased. He doesn't want nonchalant followers who are familiar with His ways. He wants vibrant followers that are surprised at His every move. God likes surprising us. He loves to see us smile. God loves seekers.

It is the glory of God to conceal a thing: but the honour of kings is to search out a matter. (Proverbs 25:2)

God loves playing hard to get, not for the purpose of prolonging blessings, but for the purpose of filtering out the fakes. See the search is a test, that every Believer must pass. It is the test of the search. God will walk through fire, just to see if you are going to follow Him.

As the deer pants for streams of water, so my soul pants for you, O God. (Psalm 42:1 **NIV**)

The writer here says, just as the deer longs for water, that is how our soul longs for God. Is God an after thought? Is God a luxury, or a necessity? Is God someone that you need, or is He just a part of your Christian lifestyle? The reason God hasn't invaded most of our lives is because He is not a priority. God's presence must become a priority.

Thou wilt shew me the path of life: in thy presence is fulness of joy; at thy right hand there are pleasures for evermore. (Psalm 16:11)

The presence of God is not an event. God's presence is packed with benefits.

Bless the LORD, O my soul, and forget not all his benefits: (Psalm 103:2)

The presence of God is loaded with benefits: strength, clarity, peace, health, prosperity, revelation, and prophetic sight, just to name a few. What benefits have you experienced by being a chaser of His presence? When you make God's presence a priority in your life, your life will have to accommodate His presence. Drama has to leave a presence filled life. Sickness has to leave a presence filled life. There are some things that we are praying for God to change, but they will only change when His presence fills that place. God has the power to fill the voids in your life.

Yet through the scent of water it will bud, and bring forth boughs like a plant. (Job 14:9)

Real presence seekers are never dismayed by life, nor are they discouraged by failure. People who actively chase God understand resurrection power. People who chase God are never at a disadvantage, because even when the circumstance says "no", our worship says "yes." Your worship must be consistent. Never allow the rhythm of your worship to be dictated by the circumstances of your life. Worship must become your lifeline, and cultivating a life of worship must be your greatest pleasure.

I will bless the LORD at all times: his praise shall continually be in my mouth. (Psalm 34:1)

MEDITATION

Concept: The Altar (Leviticus 6:13)

When it comes to worship, the altar is irreplaceable. In the days of Old, the altar was a designated spot, pillar, or place where sacrifices where made. Throughout the Patriarchal period, the priesthood belonged to fathers. The head male of every house offered sacrifices for the house, and assumed the responsibility of worship and spiritual leadership. One of the major components of communing with God was the altar. It was the altar that established a set order for worship. It was the altar where sins were forgive. It was at the altar where God's fire would fall. The altar didn't have to be a group of rocks, but a moment in which the worshipper surrendered to God. Whenever you surrender to God, you are building God an altar.

Take a moment and think about times you've built an altar to the Lord. Do you have a dedicated spot where you and God meet? Do you have a dedicated time to spend with Jesus? Where is your altar located in your house? Do you have a consecrated room just for your encounters with the Holy One? Take a few moments and ponder on building a meeting place for you and God.

Scripture Reading:
Leviticus 6:8-18, Psalm 42, 1 Kings 18:15-25

ACTIVATION

Today your assignment is to consecrate a spot in your home, office, or even car? to serve as your altar. This spot will remain holy at all cost, and be a place where you and God convene. Make sure that this spot is anointed, and clear from distraction and noise. Limit the traffic in this space. Let this room be filled with the fragrance of worship. Nothing should happen in this room, but worship. This is your assignment.

Notes

Day 40

💡 INSPIRATION

Welcome to the last session of The Journey. As we conclude this session on the presence, I want you to be particularly prayerful. The presence of God is not an event. The presence of God is not a feeling. While there are events that highlight His presence, and while there are times where we feel His presence strong, the presence of God can not be reduced to an event. The presence of God can not be shrunk down to goosebumps and feelings. The presence of God is our inheritance.

And the LORD spake unto Aaron, Thou shalt have no inheritance in their land, neither shalt thou have any part among them: I am thy part and thine inheritance among the children of Israel (Numbers 18:20).

When the Promised Land was divided among the 12 tribes of Israel, there was one group of people that did not get land, the Levites. The tribe of Levi was dedicated to serving God, and the temple. Their lives were totally devoted to the upkeep of the temple, and the spiritual affairs of Israel. The Levites didn't have a place to plant and grow crops, they ate what God provided out of the offerings. The Levites totally dedicated their lives to serving God. God wasn't their job, God was their portion. God wasn't their "plan B." God was all they had. It's easy to forget that sometimes. God is not an option, He is your only hope. Our worship must reflect this reality. Our worship must reflect the fact that God is all we have. The presence of God is our portion as priests.

But ye are a chosen generation, a royal priesthood, an holy nation, a peculiar people; that ye should shew forth the praises of him who hath called you out of darkness into his marvellous light: (1 Peter 2:9)

The scripture says that we are a "royal priesthood." We belong to a nation of priests. Jesus, by His blood, has made us both kings and priests (Rev. 1:5-6). This is a great theology truth, that we are all priests. What does this mean? God has called each of us to forsake the things of the world, and commit to Him and His presence. The presence of God is not an after thought, but our number one priority. We will be a generation that goes after the glory of God. YOU JUST SHIFTED GEARS. This is not the end, but only the beginning. I AM A GOD CHASER (repeat 7 times aloud)! The presence of God is your portion. "Glory and honour are in his presence; strength and gladness are in his place" (1 Chron. 16:27). God's presence is our reward. Our recompense is the presence of God. The highest honor is for God to give us His presence. One of the secrets to courting the presence of God is spontaneous worship. The same way that your partner surprises you with gifts when you are dating, God is the same way. As we conclude The Journey, we close out by making a commitment to the presence of God. We are glory carriers, and defenders of the presence of God. God's presence is not something that happens when we lift our hands. We lift our hands because we desperately need His presence. "I will therefore that men pray every where, lifting up holy hands, without wrath and doubting" (1 Tim. 2:8).

Regardless of where you are right now, can you lift your hands and begin to give God glory?

MEDITATION

Do the difficult things while they are easy and do the great things while they are small. A journey of a thousand miles must begin with a single step.
-Lao Tzu

Today I want you to ponder on what The Journey has meant to you. How did you enjoy it? What did you learn? Were you consistent? Take a few moments and think about some of the awesome moments created by The Journey. Did it stretch you? What was your overall experience like? Here are some question you should answer:

1. Did I complete every day of The Journey?
2. Would this be something I would do again, with more commitment?
3. Do I need a mentor?
4. Am I clear about my calling, purpose, and destiny?
5. What steps should I take to keep this development ongoing?

Take a few moments and ponder these question, and jot your answers down.

ACTIVATION

Today your activation is simple. Buy a BRAND NEW copy of The Journey, and give it to a friend. YOUR JOUNEY is just beginning.

Notes

_____
_____
_____
_____
_____

Notes

THE JOURNEY

Made in the USA
Middletown, DE
21 December 2017